MĀORI PLACE NAMES

MĀORI PLACE NAMES

THEIR MEANINGS AND ORIGINS

• FOURTH EDITION •

✕

A.W. REED

— REVISED BY **PETER DOWLING** —

Oratia

Published by Oratia Books, Oratia Media Ltd, 783 West Coast Road, Oratia, Auckland 0604, New Zealand/Aotearoa (www.oratia.co.nz).

Copyright © 2016 A.W. Reed Estate
Copyright © 2016 Oratia Books (published work)

The copyright holders assert their moral rights in the work.

This book is copyright. Except for the purposes of fair reviewing, no part of this publication may be reproduced or transmitted in any form or by any means, whether electronic, digital or mechanical, including photocopying, recording, any digital or computerised format, or any information storage and retrieval system, including by any means via the Internet, without permission in writing from the publisher. Infringers of copyright render themselves liable to prosecution.

ISBN 978-0-947506-08-7

First published as *Maori Place Names and their Meanings* 1950
First published as *A Dictionary of Maori Place Names* 1961
Reprinted 1963, 1969, 1972, 1974, 1978
Second edition 1982
Reprinted 1983, 1985, 1986, 1987, 1988, 1990, 1991, 1992, 1994
Third edition published as *The Reed Dictionary of Māori Place Names* 1996
Reprinted successively
Fourth edition published 2016

Revising editor: Peter Dowling
Consulting editor: Ross Calman
Editorial assistant: Elisa Tinti
Pre-production: Arantxa Zecchini Dowling
Cover design: Spencer Levine
Page design: IslandBridge

Printed in China

Contents

Foreword to the 2016 edition	7
Foreword to the 1961 edition	9
Hints on pronunciation	12
Key words in Māori place names	13
Māori place names	15
Appendix: European place names	147

MAPS

Te Ika-a-Māui (North Island)	inside front cover
Te Waipounamu (South Island)	inside back cover

Foreword
to the 2016 edition

Nau mai ki tēnei whakatakotoranga o ngā ingoa wāhi Māori o Aotearoa.

Aotearoa New Zealand is noted for its rich blend of English and Māori place names (ingoa wāhi). The appreciation of ingoa wāhi Māori – at times poetic, at others simply descriptive – has been a distinguishing feature of our history; European settlers often favoured original names over later imports. With time the acceptance of Māori alternatives to English names has also increased.

The previous edition added macrons to long vowels where required. Macrons make all the difference to a name's meaning and pronunciation. Few official place names carry macrons as yet, so flexibility is needed when relating the names listed here to those encountered on maps or signs.

In this edition I undertook to update usage as it has evolved over the past 20 years, resulting in revision to numerous entries. There is now more prominent reference to the Māori names of main centres, with inclusion of some important localities (such as Tūrangawaewae), regions (like Te Upoko-o-Te-Ika), and coastal and marine names (like Te Tai-o-Marokura). Additional cross-referencing and maps inside the cover aim to make the book easier to navigate. Revisions have been made to a number of factual and grammatical issues.

This edition separately classifies names starting with the letters 'ng' and 'wh'. Reed had previously favoured inclusion of those names under 'n' and 'w', but most dictionaries and other reference sources now acknowledge the Māori alphabet in grouping definitions. So for Ngāruawāhia or Whanganui, look respectively under 'Ng and 'Wh'.

My thanks to the Reed Trust for their help and encouragement, and for permitting the inclusion of the illustrations by James Berry that featured in the 1950 edition. James Berry was an outstanding artist whose vignettes helpfully illuminate aspects of the text.

Thanks also to the team who have brought this fourth edition together. Consulting editor Ross Calman and designer Graeme Leather provided invaluable knowledge and experience with Reed books, while Spencer Levine, Elisa Tinti and Arantxa Zecchini Dowling brought sharp, fresh eyes.

Useful resources for those interested in further study of the field are H.W. Williams' *Dictionary of the Maori Language* and P.M. Ryan's *The Raupō Dictionary of Modern Māori*; A.W. Reed & Peter Dowling's *Place Names of New Zealand* (Penguin, 2010); the wallchart *Aotearoa New Zealand: An Introduction to Māori Place Names and Iwi* (Reed, 2003); and the Te Ara online encyclopedia.

Toi te kupu, toi te mana, toi te whenua.

Peter Dowling
Ōrātia, April 2016

Foreword
to the 1961 edition

This book is the successor to *Maori Place Names and their Meanings*, which was first published in 1950 and which has been reprinted a number of times. It is now felt that the time has come when it should be completely revised, and enlarged by the inclusion of more factual material than the earlier book was able to provide.

A personal word of explanation may not be out of place. *Maori Place Names and their Meanings* was compiled by the present author because of the need that had been expressed for a book of this kind. Information was sought from obvious sources such as the *New Zealand Official Year Book* for 1919, in which the late Elsdon Best had given a brief list of meanings of Māori names; Mr Johannes C. Andersen's *Maori Place Names*; Mr G.G.M. Mitchell's *Maori Place Names of Buller County*, and other works that were readily accessible.

It was realised at the time that there are many problems to be faced in attempting a literal translation of Maori place names, many of which go back to early days; some indeed were used in the homeland of Hawaiki and transplanted to the soil of Aotearoa (New Zealand). Others had their origins in history and legend and have been lost, or are too long to recount in a small book. Some names have suffered alteration and distortion; some are modern names; some are too easily translated, giving false and ludicrous conclusions; and some are quite untranslatable.

On the other hand the Maori was closer to nature than the Pakeha (white man); common words for wood and water, wind and cloud and soil were frequently incorporated in his names. Common sense and direct translation provided most of the answers in the original collection, although it was always acknowledged that a more comprehensive and documented work would eventually be required.

As it happened, the task of putting together the first reference book was the start of a fascinating hobby, which has resulted in a collection of the origins of place names in New Zealand. The fruits of some of this work will be found in the present book.

The information contained in *Maori Place Names* has been gathered from hundreds of books, and through correspondence and conversation with many who are able to provide specialised knowledge in different parts of the country.

Some of the limitations of the first collection still apply, for a really satisfactory answer can seldom be supplied to the question 'What does this name mean?' The Pakeha reader will realise how futile it would be to attempt to translate English names in New Zealand for the benefit of Maori readers; what would he make, for instance, of such names as Gore, Nightcaps, Huntly, Cashmere, Fortrose, Dunedin, Auckland, Shotover and Drury? A similar problem faces us when we attempt to make a literal translation of Maori names.

On the other hand, sufficient historical and legendary tradition has been preserved to enable us to say with some certainty how some names were determined, and to give their meanings. We trust that the interested reader may find interesting glimpses of Maori life in the short notes that are attached to some of the names.

In order to assist the reader, the names have been broken up into their several components, with a translation of the words that these comprise. If sense can be made of the resulting words, a meaning has been attempted. But it must be emphasised that this meaning is no more than an attempt at translating a word, a phrase or a sentence from one language to another. The interested reader who is equipped with a Maori dictionary may himself arrive at an equally satisfying translation.

A comprehensive selection of names has been made, but a large volume would be required to include every Maori place. All the best-known and more important Maori names are included, but there is also a selection of older names, which are no longer in use, but which most readers may come across at some time or another — an obvious example is Aorangi, the Maori name for Mount Cook. Some lesser-known names are mentioned because of the interest attached to their origin.

The appendix consists of Pakeha names to which reference is made in the text. These may be Pakeha names that have replaced the original Maori name, or Maori place names in towns and cities; e.g., under Wellington will be found references to the suburbs of Hataitai and Rongotai, which are listed in the main part of the book.

Some thought has been spent on the question of giving an indication of the location of the various places, but it is felt that this is outside the scope of the present book. Such a gazetteer would suffer through the absence of Pakeha names and by the frequent duplication of Maori names, e.g., Wairoa, found again and again in various parts of New Zealand.

It is hoped that this excursion into the meanings of Maori place names will prove stimulating to the reader, who may well be encouraged to make his own investigations. To assist those who are interested, or who may require the meaning of a name of some place not included in this book, a list of words that commonly form a part of Maori place names will be found at the beginning of the book. Readers who wish to extend their interest in the subject are recommended to *Reeds' Concise Maori Dictionary*; those whose studies carry them further would be well advised to seek Williams' *Dictionary of the Maori Language*.

A.W. Reed
Te Whanganui-a-Tara, 1961

Hints
on pronunciation

There are fifteen letters in the Māori alphabet:

A E H I K M N NG O P R T U W and **WH**.

Every syllable in Māori ends in a vowel, which makes the proportion of vowels to consonants much higher than in English. The vowel sounds are therefore of great importance. The following list is a key guide:

A is always pronounced as the a in 'rather'.

E is always pronounced as the e in 'ten'.

I is always pronounced like the ee in 'seen'.

O is always pronounced like the o in 'border'.

U is always pronounced like the oo in 'bloom'.

When two vowels come together each is given its proper sound. The compound consonants *ng* and *wh* are the two stumbling blocks in the way of correct pronunciation. The sound *ng* is that of the middle *ng* in the word 'singing'. Note that in the South Island the *ng* is usually replaced by *k*; for example, Aorangi becomes Aoraki.

Wh is usually pronounced as *f*. This is not the correct sound, which has been described as *f*, but without letting the top teeth touch the lower lip. If you can't manage this, the sound of *f* will pass muster.

Using a macron – a straight line over a vowel – makes that vowel longer. In the past this has been indicated by a double vowel. Thus 'ā' is pronounced as 'aa', 'ē' as 'ee' and so forth. Pronouncing a long vowel correctly changes the meaning of a component word and may affect how well a name is understood.

These are simple rules, but they will go a long way to helping with the correct pronunciation and understanding of Māori names.

Words
that commonly form part of Māori place names

Ahi fire.
Ao cloud.
Ara path, road.
Ata shadow.
Atua god.
Au current.
Awa river, channel, gully, valley.
Haka dance.
Hau wind.
Hua fruit, egg.
Ika fish.
Iti small.
Kai food, eat.
Kino bad.
Mā white, clear.
Mā (short for manga).
Manga branch, tributary, stream.
Mānia plain.
Manu bird.

Mata headland, point, surface, eye, raw.
Matā flint, quartz, obsidian.
Mātā heap, plant.
Maunga mountain.
Moana sea, lake.
Motu island.
Muri end, breeze.
Mutu ended, finished.
Nui big, plenty of.
O of.
Ō the place of.
One mud, sand, beach.
Pā fortified village, clump, flock.
Pae ridge, resting place.
Papa broad, flat, ground covered with vegetation.
Pō night.
Poto short.

Puke hill.

Puna spring of water.

Rangi sky.

Rau hundred, many, leaf.

Riki small, few.

Roa long, high.

Roto lake, inside.

Rua cave, hollow, two.

Tahi one, single.

Tai sea, coast, tide.

Tapu forbidden, sacred.

Tea white, clear.

Wai water.

Waka canoe.

Whanga bay, harbour, inlet, stretch of water.

Whare house.

Whata raised platform for storing food.

Whenua land, country.

A

Ahaura Probably a corrupt form of Ō-hauroa. *Ō* (the place of); *hauroa* (height). As the township of Ahaura is on an elevation, and local Māori say that the name means a cliff, the meaning is probably The place of a cliff.

Ahiaruhe *ahi* (fire); *aruhe* (fern-root). Fire for roasting fern-root. Fern-root was an important food for the Māori. It was roasted over a fire and pounded with wooden beaters.

Ahikiwi *ahi* (fire); *kiwi* (flightless bird). Fire on which kiwi were cooked.

Ahimanawa *ahi* (fire); *manawa* (heart). A chief named Tārewa-a-rua was slain by his enemies. His heart was torn out, cooked, and eaten. The Ahimanawa Range has a similar origin in the revenge of the chief Te Kohipipi. The range is in full Te Ahi-manawa-a-Te-Kohipipi (The fire of the heart of Te Kohipipi).

Ahipara *ahi* (fire); *para* (various roots used for food). Fire for roasting fern-root.

Ahitarakihi *ahi* (fire); *tarakihi* (a type of fish). Fire at which the tarakihi was roasted.

Ahitītī *ahi* (fire); *tītī* (mutton bird). Fire for cooking mutton birds.

Ahuahu To heap up. This is the Māori name for Great Mercury Island. Paikea came to this island on the back of a whale. He was cold and heaped the warm sand over him, and from this event he gave the island its name.

Ahuriri Named after Tūāhuriri, who found the lagoon blocked so that the flood destroyed the shellfish. He organised a working party to clear a channel to the sea, and the area was named after him. An alternative is 'fierce rushing', an allusion to the swift current where the river runs into the sea.

Ahuroa *ahu* (heap or mound); *roa* (long). Long mound.

Akaaka Fibrous roots.

Ākarana The Māori transliteration of Auckland.

Akaroa *aka* (South Island form of *whanga*: harbour); *roa* (long). Long harbour.

Akatārawa The original form

of the name may have been Akatārewa. *Aka* (vine); *tārewa* (trailing). Trailing vines.

Akatore   The correct form is Akatōrea. *Aka* (South Island form of *whanga*: harbour); *tōrea* (oystercatcher). Oystercatcher harbour.

Akeake   A native tree.

Akerama   This is the Māori form of the name Aceldama, 'field of blood', the name given at the time the first missionaries came to North Auckland.

Ākitio   *āki* (to smash); *tio* (piercing cold). It is said that the name came from a famous greenstone mere (club).

Amokura   The name of a tropical bird that visits New Zealand. It is distinguished by two brilliant red tail-feathers. The name was given in 1929.

Amuri   Correctly, Haumuri, which means an east wind, or 'the wind at your back'.

Anakiwa   *ana* (cave); *a* (of); *Kiwa* (a man's name). Kiwa was also one of the gods of the ocean. The cave of Kiwa.

Anatoki   *ana* (cave); *toki* (adze). Cave of the adze.

Anaura   This may be a name that has come from Mangaia in the Cook Islands. In a true Māori form it would be Anakura. *Ana* (cave); *kura* (red). Red cave.

Anawhakairo   *ana* (cave); *whakairo* (to paint or carve in a pattern). Cave of carved or sculptured rock. In a cave on the banks of the Waitaki River near Coal Creek, the water has carved out recesses, pinnacles and holes in the rock.

Anawhata   *ana* (cave); *whata* (food-store). Cave of the food-store.

Āniwaniwa   Rainbow.

Aohanga   A variety of flax. The name has appeared at various times as Ohonga, Ohanga, and Aohanga, but the official name is now Ōwahanga. *Ō* (the place of); *wahanga* (entrance, mouth). The name was applied to the whole river.

Toki: adze

Aokaparangi *ao* (cloud); *kapa* (row or rank); *rangi* (sky). A row of clouds in the sky.

Aokautere *ao* (cloud); *kautere* (to float or move swiftly). Swiftly moving clouds.

Aongatete *ao* (cloud); *ngatete* (to move). Moving clouds.

Aoraki/Aorangi *ao* (cloud); *rangi* (sky). Cloud in the sky. Māori name for Mount Cook, the highest mountain peak in the country. It is popularly translated as Sky-piercer, but this is incorrect. South Island Māori call it Aoraki, because *raki* is the South Island pronunciation of *rangi*. The name is applied to many other parts of New Zealand and sometimes it has an entirely different origin.

Aorere *ao* (cloud or mist); *rere* (flying). Flying mist. Te Tai-o-Aorere, the name for Tasman Bay, means The coast of flying foam.

Aoroa *ao* (cloud); *roa* (long). Long cloud.

Aotea The name of the canoe in which Turi came to New Zealand. The Aotea gave its name to a small harbour on the west coast of the North Island where the immigrants first landed. It is also the Māori name for Great Barrier Island. There is a farming district in Marlborough named Aotea by Archdeacon Grace because it means sunny spot.

Aotearoa The usual meaning given to the Māori name for New Zealand is Land of the long white cloud. *Ao* (cloud); *tea* (white); *roa* (long). But the following interpretations have also been given by various authorities: Long white cloud; Continuously clear light; Big glaring light; Land of abiding day; Long white world; Long bright world; Long daylight; Long lingering day; Long bright land; Long bright day.

When Kupe, the discoverer of New Zealand, first came in sight of the land, his wife cried, 'He ao! He ao!' (A cloud! A cloud!). Great Barrier Island was named Aotea (white cloud), and the long mainland Aotearoa (long white cloud).

Aotuhia *ao* (daylight); *tuhia* (to glow). Glowing daylight.

Aowhenua *ao* (daylight); *whenua* (land or country). Land of daylight.

Aparima *apa* (a party of workmen); *rima* (five). The Māori name for Riverton is almost certainly that of a celebrated

Waitaha chieftainess of long ago. Other possible explanations are the Māori form of Apolima, an island in the Pacific; 'five-fold streams'; or 'five-fold ridges'.

Āpiti   Narrow pass or gorge.

Apoka   This small Marlborough inlet is named after a man, Apoka, who lived there.

Aponga   Gathered together or heaped up.

Ara-a-kiwa   The path of Kiwa. The Māori name for Foveaux Strait. Kiwa was an ocean god.

Arahiwi   *ara* (track or path); *hiwi* (ridge or hill-top). A descriptive name. Path over the ridge.

Arahura   *ara* (path); *hura* (to discover). The name is connected with Ngahue, who accompanied Kupe on his voyage of exploration down to the West Coast of the South Island. Ngahue gave the name to commemorate their search. Another origin may be with Ara'ura, the ancient name of Aitutaki in the Cook Islands.

Arahura was an early name for the South Island.

Ārai   Screen or veil.

Ārai-te-uru   The name of the early canoe that was wrecked at Moeraki. Originally applied to Shag Point (Matakaea).

Arakihi   *ara* (path); *kihi* (to be cut off).

Aramataī   *ara* (path); *mataī* (native tree). The path indicated by a mataī tree.

Aramiro   *ara* (path); *miro* (native tree). This and the previous name may indicate that a path was made across a stream by felling a tree.

Aramoana   *ara* (path); *moana* (ocean).

Aramoho   The correct form is Aramuhu. *Ara* (path); *muhu* (to force one's way through heavy bush). A man named Hau-e-rangi was lost in the dense bush here and wandered about until he died of starvation. When his body was found it was seen that he had beaten an almost circular path in his struggle to find a way out.

Aranui   The origin of this name varies for different places. In Christchurch it was probably from *ara* (path); *nui* (big).

The Aranui Cave at Waitomo was named after a man who discovered it while pig-hunting.

The Aranui Creek on the West Coast derives from *ara* (a small, freshwater fish); *nui* (many). Large numbers of grayling were taken in this creek by Māori.

Aranga   The act of rising.

Arapaepae *ara* (path); *paepae* (ridge). Path along a ridge.

Arapaoa *ara* (path); *paoa* (smoke, or blow). This is the correct form of Arapawa Island, but was also used for the whole of the South Island, and later for the island where Captain Cook landed in Cook Strait. It was here, close to the entrance of Queen Charlotte Sound, that Kupe with a downward blow (paoa) killed the enormous octopus Muturangi. Another theory is that early Māori peered through the mist across the strait, which they called 'the misty path'.

Arapawa *ara* (path); *Pawa* (name of Kupe's slave). Arapawa Island, however, is correctly spelt Arapaoa, q.v.

Arapito *ara* (path); *pito* (end). Māori travelled along a well-used track by the Karamea River inland to snare birds and gather berries. The track ended at a point where the present settlement of Arapito stands.

Arapōhue *ara* (path); *pōhue* (convolvulus plant). Path through the convolvulus.

Arapuni *ara* (path); *puni* (blocked, or place of encampment). The meaning may be Path to the camp, or a path that has been blocked up by some obstruction.

Ararātā *ara* (path); *rātā* (native tree). Path by or through rātā trees.

Ararimu *ara* (path); *rimu* (native tree). Path by or through rimu trees.

Rimu: native tree

Ararua *ara* (path); *rua* (two). Two paths.

Arataha *ara* (path); *taha* (to pass by).

Aratapu *ara* (path); *tapu* (sacred, or prohibited). The sacred path, or Path to a sacred place. The full name is Te Aratapu-o-Manaia. Manaia was a chief who came to New Zealand in the Tokomaru canoe around the thirteenth century and landed here on the Wairoa River, Kaipara.

Aratāura Probably derived from *ara* (path); *tāuru* (head or source of a stream). Path by the source of a stream.

Aratiatia *ara tiatia* (a series of pegs stuck into the ground to assist in climbing a steep ascent). This descriptive name has been applied to the rapids on the Waikato River because the water seems to zig-zag from one rock to another. It may be connected with the explorer Tia, who proceeded up the rapids in his small canoe, criss-crossing up a series of small ledges.

Aratika *ara* (path); *tika* (straight). Direct path.

Aratoro *ara* (path); *toro* (to explore, to discover).

Arawhata This may mean a hanging path. A *whata* is a food-store elevated on a post to keep the contents away from rats. Such stores were sometimes approached by a notched post that was leant against the store, thus providing a series of steps or stairs. Such a stairway was known as an arawhata, a path to the food-store.

Arero Tongue. There is a tradition that there was a battle here, and that the victors cut out the tongues of the vanquished.

Āria A deep pool, or a stretch of water suitable for fishing by net.

Ariki-kapakapa *ariki* is short for *puna-ariki* (hot springs); *kapakapa* (flapping). The name refers to the flapping or fluttering noise made by the hot spring.

Aroaro-kaihe The Māori name for Mount Sefton. Aroaro-kaihe and her husband Mauka-tū (Ben Ōhau) were both members of the crew of the Ārai-te-uru canoe.

Aropaoanui *aro* (fat covering the kidneys); *paoa nui* (thoroughly bashed). The pā at the mouth of the Aropaoanui river was raided, but the defenders were victorious. After they had cooked their slain enemies, the bodies were seen still to be moving. Their chief realised it was the kidney fat twitching and thoroughly bashed the offending portions.

Arorangi *aro* (front); *rangi* (heaven). The front of heaven. The name was brought from Tahiti.

Arowhenua *aro* (face or front); *whenua* (land). Several interpretations have been given from time to time, including Good or desirable land; Turning up land for cultivation; and To face or desire land. An ancient Polynesian name transplanted to New Zealand, it is occasionally used to refer to Invercargill.

Ātaahua   Good, beautiful, or pleasant.

Atapō   *ata* (shadow); *pō* (night). Night shadows. A name for the dark time just before dawn.

Atarau   Moon, or moonlight.

Atawhai   Liberality, or kindness.

Ātea   Space. A synonym for Wātea, the personified form of space.

Ātene   The Māori form of Athens. The name was given to the mission station on the Whanganui River by the Reverend Richard Taylor, the original Māori name being O-a-whiti.

Ātiamuri   It was at the Ātiamuri Rapids that Tia, the elder brother of the commander of the Arawa canoe, turned back. The name therefore can be broken up into the words Ā-Tia-muri, muri here meaning 'turned back'.

It has also been conjectured that the word is a contraction of the tribal name Ngāti a Muri.

Atiu   One of the oldest names in Marlborough, it has probably been transferred from the Cook Islands.

Auripo   Both *au* and *ripo* mean whirlpool or swirling current.

Auroa   *au* (cloud, mist, or current); *roa* (long).

Awaawaroa   *awaawa* (valley); *roa* (long). Long valley.

Awahōhonu   *awa* (river); *hōhonu* (deep). Deep river.

Awahou   *awa* (river); *hou* (new). New river. The Awahou River, which flows into Lake Rotorua, was named by the explorer Īhenga.

Awahuri   *awa* (river); *huri* (barrier to turn fish into a weir). River with a weir in it.

Awaiti   *awa* (stream); *iti* (small). The name was given to a location and river in Awarua Bay, Nelson, to complement the name of the larger river in the bay, Awanui (big river).

Awakaponga   *awa* (stream); *kaponga* (tree-fern). Tree-fern stream.

Awakari   *awa* (river); *kari* (isolated clump of trees). River with isolated patches of bush on the banks.

Awakeri   Ditch.

Awakino   *awa* (river); *kino* (bad). Bad river. The Awakino River is still muddy in places, which possibly gave rise to the name.

Awakōkōmuka   See Awamoa.

Awamangu   *awa* (river); *mangu* (black). Black river.

Awamarino   *awa* (river); *marino* (calm). Calm river.

Awamate   *awa* (river); *mate* (dead). Dead river, or Former river. At Awamate in Nelson, a branch of the Motueka River used to run through the place that bore this name.

Awamoa   *awa* (stream); *moa* (large, extinct flightless bird). Moa stream. The name was given by W.B.D. Mantell in about 1852. The original name was Awakōkōmuka. Awa (stream); kōkōmuka (the South Island name for koromiko: a native species of veronica). At the mouth of the stream Mantell discovered ancient ovens of the Waitaha tribe containing moa bones.

Awamōkihi   *awa* (river); *mōkihi* (a craft made of flax stalks). The stream north of Ōamaru was named after a man called Awamōkihi.

Awamoko   *awa* (stream); *moko* (lizard). Lizard stream.

Awanui   *awa* (river); *nui* (large, or many). The name may have been brought from Hawaiki.

Awanga   South-west wind, or a variety of flax or taro.

Awapuni   *awa* (river); *puni* (blocked up). It has been suggested that the river may have been blocked up with driftwood when it was named.

There was a lagoon called Te Awapuni at Palmerston North, which was an ox-bow or cut-off river bend, and could thus be described as a blocked river.

Awapūtakitaki   *awa* (river); *pūtakitaki* (the South Island form of *pūtangitangi*: Paradise duck).

Awarere   *awa* (river); *rere* (flowing). Flowing river.

Awariki   *awa* (river); *riki* (small). Small river.

Awaroa   *awa* (river); *roa* (long). Long river.

Moa: extinct bird

Awarua *awa* (river); *rua* (two). Two rivers, or arms. The name is a common one in New Zealand and throughout Polynesia. Avarua is the name of a harbour in Ra'iatea, which had two openings in the reef.

Awatea Daylight, or midday.

Awatere *awa* (river); *tere* (swift flowing). Swift-flowing river. Of the river at East Cape it is said that in a battle one man had his stomach ripped open, and the contents ran swiftly down the current, hence the name.

The name may be the true form of Kawatiri.

Awatoitoi *awa* (river); *toitoi* (a small freshwater fish, a variety of flax, or possibly a corruption of toetoe).

Awatoto *awa* (river); *toto* (blood), or *tōtō* (the name of a ceremony performed over a child, usually by the side of a stream).

Awatuna *awa* (creek); *tuna* (eel). Eel creek. The settlement of this name in Taranaki is known locally as Eels Creek.

Āwhitu Longing to return. Literally the meaning of āwhitu is to feel regret for, to yearn for. At one time the people at this settlement near the heads of the Manukau Harbour were forced to abandon their pā because of the depredations of the taniwha Kaiwhare, and the place was named because of their longing to return to the land they loved.

Eaheinomauwe Captain Cook's spelling of the Māori name for the North Island; also Aeheinomouwe. It probably stands for *He Ahi nō Māui* (The fire of Māui), and refers to the volcanoes of the central plateau.

Ekemānuka *eke* (to make one's way through); *mānuka* (tea-tree). A party of Māori who were out hunting saw a large enemy force approaching. They made their escape unseen by crouching down and creeping through the short mānuka scrub.

Eketāhuna *eke* (to run aground); *tāhuna* (shoal or sandbank). This place was as far as the Makakahi River could be navigated by canoes on account of the shoals.

Epuni Correctly Te Puni. Te Puni was one of the leaders of the Te Āti Awa settlement of Te Whanganui-a-Tara (Wellington) after migrating south with Te Rauparaha.

Erua Two. The *e* is a particle used before digits one to nine in enumeration, e.g., e rua, e toru, two, three. Possibly a misspelling of He rua, a cave. Another ingenious explanation of the name is E rua!, which could be translated colloquially, 'There's a cave!'.

Haehaenui *haehae* (to lacerate, or parallel grooves in a carving); *nui* (big). This is the original name for the Arrow River; it means 'big scratches' — a reference to the number of channels the river has carved.

Haerehuka *haere* (to come or go); *huka* (foam). The name was apparently applied to the great rock in the middle of the Huka Falls. It has been popularly translated Moving foam, or Flying foam.

Hairini Possibly the Māori form of Ireland, but more probably it is a missionary name, Cyrene, which takes this form in Māori.

Hakahaka The name of a Marlborough chief.

Hakakura *haka* (a South Island form of *whanga*: a stretch of water); *kura* (red). Reddish-coloured hollow. It is the original Māori name for Lake Sumner.

Hākana This bay at Port Underwood is, in a roundabout way, probably named after the pioneer missionary the Reverend Samuel Ironside. He was known to Māori as Haeana, which was the Māori transliteration of 'iron'. Hākana may be a corruption of Haeana.

Hakapōua *haka* (South Island form of *whanga*: stretch of water); *pōua* (old man). The name has been translated as Old Man Gulf.

Hakapūpū *haka* (South Island form of *whanga*: harbour); *pūpū* (several kinds of shellfish). Estuary of the shellfish.

Hakapūreirei *haka* (dance); *pūreirei* (tufts of grass, or small patch of garden).

Hakarū *haka* (dance); *rū* (to shake).

Hakataramea *haka* (dance); *taramea* (spear-grass). The name commemorates a dance that took place near the mouth of the river. The performers wore bags filled with the sweet-scented gum from the flower stalks of the taramea. The bags in which the gum was contained were made from the skin of the whēkau, an owl that is now extinct.

Hakatere *haka* (a form of whaka: to make); *tere* (swift). To make swift. It is the Māori name for the Ashburton River.

Hāmama To shout aloud. Three young men from Taumarunui came down the Whanganui River and killed a chief named Tamatuna and insulted his wives. Caught by surprise, Tamatuna shouted out loudly.

Hamaria A missionary village on the shore of Lake Taupō, named after the Biblical town of Samaria.

Hamurana The Māori form of the Biblical name Smyrna, given to the springs at Rotorua, which were originally called Te Puna-a-Hangarua. See Hangarua.

Hangaroa An ornamental belt, anklet, or necklace made of shells.

Hangarua A name occasionally given to Hamurana Springs, q.v. The full name is Te Puna-a-Hangarua, meaning The spring of Hangarua. It was presided over by a taniwha or water-monster named Hinerua. The small blind fish, kōaro, which came up in the waters of the spring from time to time, were called the Children of Hinerua.

Hangatiki *hanga* (to fashion or make); *tiki* (an image in human form). To carve a wooden post in the form of a tiki.

Tiki: stylised human form

Hāparangi To shout, or to cut open.

Hāpua A hollow or pool.

Hāpuawhenua *hāpua* (depression); *whenua* (land).

Hāpuku The fish known to Pākehā as groper.

Harakeke Flax (*Phormium tenax*).

Harihari A song to make people pull together in unison.

Hātaitai The original name for the Miramar Peninsula, and the Wellington suburb. The name most likely commemorates the taniwha Whātaitai who, beaten by fellow taniwha Ngake in opening an entrance to the harvour, flew screaming to the top of Mount Victoria (Tangi-te-keo). The suburb should therefore be named Whātaitai.

There have been attempts to provide a literal translation. *Hā* (smell or breath) or *whā* (to cause or make known); *taitai* (tide), resulting in such meanings as The lapping of the tide, or The breath of the ocean.

Hātepe To cut off, or to proceed in an orderly manner.

Hātuma Possibly a personal name. It was sometimes called Whātuma. No meaning can be ascribed, but a kaumatua once stated that it referred to the discoverers of the lake who ate until they were satisfied. The name was given by Tara.

Hauhangaroa *hau* (wind); *hangaroa* (seashells).

Haumaitikitiki Also in the form Haumātiketike, it was applied to mountains such as Mount Brewster, Mount Prospect, and the Crown Range. The name is descriptive, meaning The wind blowing from the heights.

Haumātakitaki Named after a chieftainess of Otago.

Haumoana *hau* (wind); *moana* (ocean). Sea breeze.

Haunui *hau* (wind); *nui* (big). Strong wind.

Haupapa *hau* (wind); *papa* (flat). Windy flat.

Hauraki *hau* (wind); *raki* (north). Northern wind. There is a proverb about Hauraki that refers to a wind that rises moaning from the sea. No doubt this is the north wind. It has been said, however, that Hauraki (or Haurangi) was a personal name. See Tīkapa Moana.

Hauroko *hau* (wind); *roko* (South Island form of *rongo*: sound, feel, hear). Sound (or feeling) of the wind. This is the meaning ascribed to it by Southland Māori, and the name has been officially noted. But it has been the subject of dispute in the past, for it is held by some northern Māori that it should be Hauroto. *Hau* (wind); *roto* (lake). Windy lake.

Hautapu *hau* (there are many meanings; here it possibly refers to a religious ceremony); *tapu* (sacred). Sacred ceremony.

Hautekapakapa *hau* (wind); *te* (the); *kapakapa* (flapping). The flapping of the wind.

Hautere *hau* (wind); *tere* (swift). Swift wind.

Hauturu *hau* (wind); *turu* (post). Wind's resting-post. This is the Māori name for Little Barrier Island. In legend it is the centre post of the great net of Taramainuku. For an account of this net, see Te Kupenga-a-Taramainuku.

Hauwai A mollusc.

Hāwea The Hāwea tribe were among the original inhabitants of the South Island. The lake and other places where the name occurs may be named originally from one of Rākaihautū's men. If the name was given through some event in history, it implies doubt and indecision.

Hāwera *hā* (breath); *wera* (hot, or burnt). Breath of fire. The occupants of a crowded whare were attacked by their enemies here, and the house was set on fire. The people who were inside were killed by 'the breath of fire'.

He Ahi-nō-Māui An ancient name for the North Island. See Eaheinomauwe.

Heipipi *hei* (necklace); *pipi* (shellfish). Necklace of pipi.

Hekeia The father of Te Anau, one of the early immigrants from Hawaiki.

Hekura The name of a woman of the Ārai-te-uru canoe.

Hemo To cease, or disappear.

Herekino *here* (knot); *kino* (bad). Badly tied knot.

Heretaunga *here* (to tie); *taunga* (to come to rest, applied to a canoe). But Heretaunga of the Hutt Valley was never a suitable place for canoes. It has been suggested that it is a corruption of Hautonga, breath of the south wind. There is also a theory that the name was imported from Hawke's Bay. The Heretaunga Plains were named after a notable carved house built near present-day Hastings by Whātonga.

Hiapo The famous sisters Kuiwai and Haungaroa left their brother

Hiapo here while they went to Maketū to carry messages from Hawaiki to Ngātoroirangi.

Hihitahi *hihi* (stitch-bird); *tahi* (single). A single stitch-bird.

Hikuai This may be a contraction of Hikuwai, one meaning of which is Tail end of the backwash. *Hiku* (fish's tail); *wai* (water).

Hikurangi The name appears in many parts of New Zealand, because it commemorates a well-known and loved mountain peak in Hawaiki. The probable meaning is *hiku* (point, or summit); *rangi* (sky).

Hikutaiā *hiku* (tail, or end); *taiā* (neap tide). Tail end of the tide.

Hīmatangi *hī* (to fish with hook and line); *Matangi* (the name of a chief). Matangi's fishing. At one time it was thought that the name was really Hima-tangi, referring to the weeping (tangi) of Hima for her lost greenstone treasure. But the story is now believed to relate to the chief Matangi, who settled here long ago. Travellers were killed by a huge taniwha in a lake by the Manawatū River and Matangi set out with twelve men to kill it. Some of them acted as bait, tempting the taniwha from its home. Others lay in wait and snared it with ropes when it emerged, then killed it.

Hinahina A native tree.

Hinakura The name of a chieftainess who took ill and died by the Pāhaoa River. She was buried there and the place was named after her. The correct form of the name is Hinekura.

Hīnau A native tree.

Hinerua *hine* (girl); *rua* (two). Two girls.

Hine-te-awa *hine* (girl); *te* (the); *awa* (river). The girl of the river. This is the original name of Bowen Falls, which are named after a woman who lived long ago.

Hinuera Correctly, Hinuwera. *Hinu* (oil, or fat); *wera* (burning). Burning fat or oil.

Hīona A missionary name for a pā on the Whanganui River. It is the Māori form of Zion.

Hira Abundant, or multitude.

Hiruhārama Māori form of Jerusalem. Named by the Reverend Richard Taylor.

Hītaua A small waist-mat or apron.

Hiwinui *hiwi* (ridge); *nui* (big). Big ridge.

Hiwipango Correctly, Hiwiponga. *Hiwi* (ridge); *ponga* (tree-fern). Ridge covered with tree-ferns.

Hoe-o-Tainui *hoe* (paddle); *o* (of); *Tainui* (the Tainui canoe). Paddle of the Tainui canoe. Now usually Te Hoe-o-Tainui.

Hōhonu Deep. A suitable name for the river.

Hokianga It is from here that Kupe the navigator returned to Hawaiki. From this event the place was named Hokianga, Great returning place of Kupe. It is said that the correct form is Hoki-anga-nui (direct return), or Te Hokianga-nui-a-Kupe.

Hōkio Whistling. Hau gave the name because the wind whistled in his ears.

Hokitika *hoki* (to return); *tika* (directly, or in a straight line). When some of Ngāi Tahu were about to attack the pā here, one or more of their chiefs were drowned, and they therefore made a direct return back to their home. Bishop Harper wrote that the name means 'When you get there, turn back again, as the Māori regard it as the end of the earth.'

Hokonui There are two explanations. First, that *hoko* is a contraction of hokowhitu (war party); *nui* (large). Large war party. Second, that Hokonui is a corruption of hukanui. *Huka* (snow); *nui* (big). Thick snow.

Hokowhitu War party of about 140 men. Hokowhitu near Palmerston North was so named because of the men who garrisoned at Te Motu-o-Poutoa.

Homai To give to the person speaking.

Honikiwi *honi* (to nibble, or eat); *kiwi* (native flightless bird). Where the kiwi forages for food.

Hongihongi To smell. Turi of the Aotea canoe took up a handful of earth at this place and smelled it to see whether the soil was good.

Hongi's Point The pā Kororipo, where Hongi Hika carried the bodies of chiefs slain in battle, was here.

Hongi's Track Where Hongi took his canoes overland in 1822 from Rotoehu to Rotoiti on his way to attack Mokoia Island. The Māori name is Te Ara-a-Hongi.

Horahora Greatly expanded, or scattered about.

Hōreke To throw a spear.

Horoeka A native tree (lancewood).

Horoera *horo* (to swallow); *wera* (hot). To swallow hot.

Horohoro The name in full is Te

Horohoroinga-o-ngā-ringaringa-a-Tia, the place where Tia's hands were ceremonially washed. This was necessary to remove the tapu after handling the dead. Tia was the Arawa explorer who named Lake Taupō.

An alternative for the full name is Te Horohoronga-a-Tia, which refers to the swallowing of sacred food in a ceremony to remove tapu.

Horoirangi *horoi* (to wash, or cleanse); *rangi* (sky). When bad weather threatens Nelson, this mountain is covered with clouds.

Horokiwi *horo* (to run); *kiwi* (native bird). The running of the kiwi.

Horokōau *horo* (to swallow); *kōau* (shag). Te Horokōau is probably Mount Tasman, and is said to have been given this name because it resembled the swelling in the long neck of a shag when it is swallowing a fish. The name appears in several places in the South Island. It is also the name for the Cass River, and could there be interpreted as A precipitous landslip (horo) where shags congregated.

Horokōhatu *horo* (crumbling); *kōhatu* (stone). Crumbling stone.

It may be an adaptation of the name Te Horokōatū, who was on the Ārai-te-uru canoe.

Horopito A native shrub (the pepper tree). The literal meaning is Scent of the woods.

Hororātā *horo* (landslip); *rātā* (native tree).

Horotiu *horo* (to run); *tiu* (swift). Swiftly flowing. Above the junction of the Waipā, the Waikato River flowed swiftly. Until after the Waikato War the name Waikato was used only for the river below Ngāruawāhia; above it was termed the Horotiu.

Horotutu *horo* (landslip); *tutu* (native tree).

Horowhenua *horo* (slip); *whenua* (land). Great landslide. The whole district from Levin to the Ōhau

Hōteo: calabash

Hōteo River is a gravel deposit. It is a fan of detritus that has the appearance of an enormous landslide from the Tararua Range.

Hōteo A calabash.

Houhora *hou* (feather); *hora* (to spread out). Feathers spread out. Feathers were at one time spread out near the Houhora Heads to dry.

Houhou A native tree (five-finger).

Houhoupounamu *houhou* (to drill); *pounamu* (greenstone). To drill greenstone. This stream near Greytown was named from the custom of drilling greenstone and using the water of the stream in the process.

Houipapa *houi* (lacebark or ribbonwood tree); *papa* (flat). Ribbonwood flat. This is the name used by Pākehā.

Houpoto *hou* (feather); *poto* (short). Short feather.

Hōuto Ripe fruit of the pōporo tree.

Huapai *hua* (fruit); *pai* (good). Good fruit. This settlement north of Auckland was founded and named in 1912. It is a noted fruit-growing district.

Huarau *hua* (fruit); *rau* (hundred, or many). Plentiful fruit.

Huatai *hua* (product, or progeny); *tai* (tide). The name means Sea froth.

Hūhātahi *hūhā* (thigh); *tahi* (single). Only thigh. One of Tama-tū-pere's thighs was eaten at this place, on which the settlement of Rānana was later established.

Huia An extinct bird, the feathers of which were greatly prized. It was never known to be in the Karamea district (the Huia River is a tributary of the Karamea). The name was probably conferred by an early surveyor.

Huia: extinct bird

Huiarau *huia* (extinct bird); *rau* (many). Many huia birds.

Huihuikōura *huihui* (assembly); *kōura* (crayfish). Gathering of crayfish. Old Māori tell stories of walls of crayfish plastered solidly several tiers deep in the waters of Stevens Island, in Breaksea Sound.

Huinga Said to mean swamps.

Huiroa A species of fine flax.

Hui-te-rangiora Name of the great explorer and navigator of the seventh century, who is reputed to have sailed down to the Antarctic in his canoe. The district adjoining the mouth of Motueka River was named after him.

Huka Foam. The name of the great waterfall on the Waikato River below Lake Taupō is Hukanui in full.

Hukanui *huka* (foam, spray, or snow); *nui* (big). Great body of foam.

Hukapapa *huka* (snow, or frost); *papa* (flat). Frost lying on the ground.

Hukarere *huka* (spray, or foam); *rere* (flying). Flying foam. This was the high seaward bluff of Scinde Island, Napier, and in storms the spray would come right to the hilltop at this point.

Hūkerenui *hūkere* (cascade); *nui* (big). Great waterfall.

Hūnua Infertile, high country.

Huriawa *huri* (to turn round); *awa* (river). River turned round. The Waikouaiti River once entered the sea on the south side of the Huriawa Peninsula into Puketeraki Bay.

Hurimoana *huri* (to overflow); *moana* (ocean). Overflowing sea.

Huri-o-te-wai *huri* (to turn round); *o* (of); *te* (the); *wai* (water). The dividing of the water. This is the Māori name for Bishop's Peninsula on Pepin Island, which diverts the Whakapuaka stream from the tide.

Huritini *huri* (to revolve); *tini* (many). Ever circulating, or Many circles. It is a large pool of boiling muddy water at Tikitere.

Huruhuru-o-Taikawa *huruhuru* (coarse hair); *o* (of); *Taikawa* (name of a chieftainess). The local meaning, however, is The soft hair of Taikawa. She insisted that the muka or dressed flax of this part of Horowhenua was so fine that it should be called by this name.

Hurunui *huru* (hair); *nui* (big). One explanation is that the name means Flowing hair. It does have something of this appearance from the hills. It may have taken its name from the female dog, Hurunui, which Kupe was supposed to have left in charge of his discoveries. It may also refer to vegetation by the river banks.

I

Ihumātao *ihu* (nose): *mātao* (cold). Cold nose.

Ihumoana *ihu* (nose): *moana* (sea). Headland projecting into the sea.

Ihu-ngau-ana *ihu* (nose): *ngau* (bite); *ana* (verb particle). Nose bitten off. The chief Tamahaki had his nose bitten off by Kura at a battle here on the Whanganui River.

Ikamatua *ika* (fish); *matua* (parent, or fully grown). One explanation of the name is that it is a shortened form of Te Ika-a-matua, The fish of my ancestor (Māui).

Ikoraki A South Island form of Hikurangi.

Inangahua *inanga* (whitebait); *hua* (preserved by drying in the sun, or plenty of). The Inangahua River was noted for the big catches of whitebait that it yielded.

Irimahuwheri The correct name of this headland in the Buller district is Irimahuwhero. *Iri* (hanging); *mahu*, perhaps a contraction of *māhunga* (hair); *whero* (red). Hanging red hair. On the seaward side of the headland there are masses of rātā trees, which are sometimes ablaze with red blooms.

Iwikatea *iwi* (bone); *katea* (bleached). Bleached bones. This is the Māori name for the site of Balclutha. A great battle took place here long ago, and the bones remained unburied for many years.

Iwirua *iwi* (bone); *rua* (pit, or cave). There may have been a burial ground on this cape in Grove Arm, Marlborough Sounds.

Iwituaroa Backbone. From the sea the Iwituaroa Range bears a striking resemblance to a human backbone.

K

Kāeo Freshwater shellfish.

Kaharoa *kaha* (net); *roa* (long). Large seine or dragnet.

Kahika Native tree. Short for Kahikatea (white pine).

Kahikatea White pine. Kahikatea Bay was an early name for Curious Cove.

Kahinu This peak in the Tararua Range was named after a chief of the Rangitāne pā.

Kahiwiroa *kahiwi* (ridge); *roa* (long). Long ridge.

Kahu Named after Kahumatamomoe because he stayed here at Ōrākei in Auckland. See Ōkahu.

Kāhui Flock, or herd.

Kāhuika The meeting of the waters. It is the equivalent of the North Island Ngāhuinga, and describes the meeting of the Matau and Clutha rivers.

Kāhuikākāpō *kāhui* (meeting); *kākāpō* (ground parrot). 'Kākāpō Parliament'. An old legend says that Doubtful Sound was a place where the chief of the kākāpō sent out invitations to his subjects to meet together to discuss matters of common interest among the parrots. Spey River and Hall's Arm were similar meeting places.

Kāhuikaupeka Assembly of river-heads. The Māori name for Mount D'Archiac, which is the source of many rivers.

Kāhuikawau *kāhui* (assembly); *kawau* (shag). Assembly of shags.

Īhenga's wife exclaimed with delight at the many birds he had brought in his canoe, so the place, between Rotorua and Maketū, was given this name.

Kāhui-tamariki *kāhui* (assembly); *tamariki* (children). Assembly of children.

Kahukura Rainbow, or god of the rainbow.

Kahuranaki Properly, Kahura-a-nake, the wished for. When people set out from Wairoa to Ahuriri in their canoes, this high hill was their landmark. If it became obscured by clouds, it was greatly wished for.

Kahurangi *kahu* (blue); *rangi* (sky). Blue skies. Canoe voyagers from the North Island, Nelson and Marlborough always endeavoured to reach the mouth of the Kahurangi River in the evening, because this landfall was almost invariably associated with blue skies and calm waters.

Kahutara The name of one of the canoes in which Māori came to New Zealand. Ngāi Tahu iwi came from the North Island in a canoe with the same name and established themselves here, a little south of Kaikōura.

Kahuwera *kahu* (garment);

wera (burnt). Burnt garment. The Māori village in the Bay of Islands was so named because a woman's garment caught fire here, and she had to rush into the sea to extinguish it. The same name in Southland comes from the name of a woman who lived there about 300 years ago.

Kaiaka   Adept, or man.

Kaiapoi   According to some sources, the correct form of the name is Kaiapohia, meaning food depot. But some South Island Māori deny this, and say that it has always been Kaiapoi. *Kai* (food); *poi* (swung). The pā was in a strategic position and adequate food supplies could be 'swung' towards it from all directions.

Kaiarero   *kai* (to bite, or eat); *arero* (tongue). Bite the tongue.

Kaiata   *kai* (food); *ata* (morning). Eat in the morning.

Kaiate   *kai* (food); *ate* (liver). Meal of liver. The livers of sharks were often eaten here.

Kaiaua   *kai* (to eat); *aua* (herring). Meal of herring.

Kaihau-o-Kupe   *kai* (eating); *hau* (wind); *o* (of); Kupe. Kupe's wind-eating. When Kupe stayed at this spot at Castlecliff it was very windy.

Kaihere   *kai* (food); *here* (to tie).

Kaihiku   *kai* (to eat); *hiku* (tail of a fish). To eat fish-tails.

Kaihinu   *kai* (food); *hinu* (fat). Rich food.

Kaihū   The full name was Kaihū-a-Īhenga. *Kai* (food); *hū* (secret); *a* (of); Īhenga (grandson of Tamatekapua). Īhenga went travelling in the far north, and his men carried some toheroa inland. While his companions were absent, he ate all the remaining supplies, and pretended he knew nothing about it. He was found out, and the place named as a reminder of his greed.

Kai-iwi   *kai* (number); *iwi* (tribe). Gathering of the tribes. Kai also means eat, and iwi means bone.

One story is that a chief ate the flesh and bones of birds; another is that food of bone was threat against an enemy tribe. It is also said a woman named Hinekoatu was killed and eaten, and her bones thrown into the stream.

And there is an amusing tale that a woman named Kiteiwi was one day eating a choice morsel of kuia (old woman). Someone asked her what she was eating, and she replied, 'The bone of a kōkako (New Zealand crow)', which was a good joke, and so the place was named Kai-iwi (eat the bone).

Kāika Village. This name, which occurs often in the South Island, is the same as the North Island *kāinga*, an unfortified village.

Kaikanohi *kai* (to eat); *kanohi* (eye). A noted warrior caught his wife with another man and swallowed her eyes as an act of revenge. Thus a point on Ellesmere Spit gained its name. Elsewhere in the South Island the name came from unworked greenstone, and was also the name of a famous mere (club).

Kāikanui *kāika* (village, also kāinga); *nui* (big). Big settlement.

Kaikohe *kai* (food); *kohe* (tree, or climbing plant).

Kaikōrai Correctly, Kaikārae. *Kai* (to eat); *kārae* (a sea bird).

Kaikōura *kai* (to eat); *kōura* (crayfish). To eat crayfish. The full name is Te Ahikaikōura-a-Tamakiterangi (or Tamatea-pōkai-whenua). This great traveller stayed here and lit a fire to cook a meal of crayfish. The name was once applied to the whole of the South Island.

Kaimāī *kai* (to eat); *māī* (preserved mussel). To eat preserved mussels.

Kaimanawa *kai* (to eat); *manawa* (heart). Heart-eater.

Kaimata *kai* (to eat); *mata* (unripe, or uncooked). To eat raw food.

Kaimātaitai *kai* (to eat); *mātaitai* (seafood). To eat seafood.

Kaimātuhi *kai* (to eat); *mātuhi* (bush wren). To eat mātuhi.

Mātuhi: bush wren

Kaimaumau *kai* (food); *maumau* (wasted). Wasted food.

Kaimiro *kai* (to eat); *miro* (native tree). To eat miro berries.

Kaimoko A man skilled in the art of tattooing. This operation was probably carried out alongside a stream of this name.

Kainamu *kai* (to eat); *namu* (sandfly). To eat sandflies. At this place on the Waiau River a man was plagued by sandflies.

He licked his hand to allay the itching and inadvertently ate a mouthful of them.

Kaingaroa *kainga* (meal); *roa* (long). Protracted meal. The name in full is Te Kaingaroa-a-Haungaroa. A priestess named Haungaroa was exploring the plains. She took so long over her meal that she was teased by her companions, and the place was called The long meal of Haungaroa. The women who made the remark were changed into cabbage-trees, which recede across the plain before travellers.

Kaipakatiti *kai* (food); *pakatiti* (defective). Inedible food.

Kaipākirikiri *kai* (food); *pākirikiri* (rock-cod). Meal of rock-cod.

Kaipara *kai* (to eat); *para* (fern-root). To eat fern-root. When Kahumatamomoe and his nephew Īhenga were visiting here, they were well fed, and amongst the food was a basket of para. They had never seen or tasted it before, and named the place after the meal.

Kaiparoro *kai* (to eat); *paroro* (bad weather). To eat bad weather. There is a flat-topped hill, and the fogs disappear when they reach it.

Kaipipi *kai* (to eat); *pipi* (shellfish). To eat pipi.

Kaipō *kai* (to eat); *pō* (night). To eat at night.

Kaipuke *kai* (to eat); *puke* (hill). The hill that was eaten. In the old whaling days several ships set out their sails to dry by Kororāreka Point, thus obscuring the hill. Quick to make a joke, the Māori called it Kaipuke.

Kaipūrua *kai* (food); *pūrua* (done in pairs). Fish caught in pairs. A person who was fishing in this tributary of the Waiau River caught two fish simultaneously.

Kairanga A company of men making a charge in battle.

Kairara *kai* (food); *rara* (spread out on a platform). Food spread out on a stage.

Kaireperepe *kai* (to eat); *reperepe* (elephant-fish). Meal of elephant-fish.

Kairua A contraction of Kopūkairua. *Kopū* (full); *kai* (food); *rua* (pit). Well-stocked food pit.

Kaitāia In full, Kaitātāia. *Kai* (food); *tātāia* (thrown about). Two women competed to see who could store away the most food. Eventually there was so much gathered together that it could not be contained in the store pits and had to be thrown away.

There is another legend to the effect that Tamatea, son of Rongokako, took vast quantities of wood pigeons here. The name of the place was changed from Orongotea to Kaitāia (food in abundance).

Kaitakata A South Island form of Kaitangata, man-eater. A party of Māori travelling along the beach near Orepuki were overwhelmed by a 'man-eating' wave.

Kaitangata *kai* (to eat); *tangata* (man). The eating of man. After a battle between two tribes over eeling rights on the lakes, the victors ate the chief Mokomoko.

Another account says that the place was named after one of the crew of the Ārai-te-uru canoe, who found a supply of paint in the hills nearby, and was skilled at using it.

Kaitangiweka *kai* (food); *tangi* (to cry); *weka* (wood-hen). The crying of the wood-hen for food.

Kaitarakihi *kai* (food); *tarakihi* (type of fish). Meal of tarakihi. The fishing ground is located by the Māori by sailing out until this mountain comes into view.

Kaitawa *kai* (to eat); *tawa* (native tree).

Kaiteretere *kai* (to eat); *teretere* (quickly). To eat in a hurry. Local Māori who were having a meal on the beach were surprised by stones rolling down the hillside. Fearing a surprise attack, they gathered their food together and ate hurriedly as they retired to the pā.

Kaitī *kai* (to eat); *tī* (cabbage-tree). To eat the leaves of the cabbage-tree.

Kaitīeke *kai* (to eat); *tīeke* (saddleback, a native bird). To eat the saddleback.

Kaitoke *kai* (to eat); *toke* (worm). The soil was very poor, and on occasion nothing could be found to eat but worms.

Kaitorete *kai* (to eat); *torete* (parakeet). To eat parakeet. The Ellesmere Spit was a place that had a plentiful supply of birds and fish for food.

Kaituna *kai* (to eat); *tuna* (eel). To eat eels. There were many localities with this name, and no doubt it was a sign that eels abounded and were a popular food.

Kaiuku *kai* (to eat); *uku* (blue clay). To eat clay. The people of this pā were beleaguered, and when their food supplies ran out, they ate clay to assuage their hunger. Their bravery and tenacity were rewarded when a taua came to their aid, the warriors being pulled up the cliff to the pā by ropes.

Kaiumu *kai* (food); *umu* (oven). Food oven.

Kaiwaiwai Correctly, Kaiwaewae. *Kai* (to eat); *waewae* (foot). Destructive to the feet. In the early days the wild Irishman shrub grew plentifully around Featherston, and took its toll on the bare feet of the Māori.

Kaiwaka *kai* (to eat); *waka* (canoe). Destroyer of canoes. Most places where this name is found are by the banks of a swiftly running river or stream, which is noted for the canoes 'eaten' or destroyed.

Kaiwharawhara *kai* (to eat); *wharawhara* (fruit of the astelia, which grows in the forks of trees). To eat wharawhara.

Kākā Native parrot.

Kākahi Freshwater mussel.

Kākaho Culm of the *toetoe* grass.

Kākahoroa *kākaho* (culm of the *toetoe*); *roa* (long). The original name for Whakatāne.

Kakanui Correctly, Kakaunui. *Kakau* (to swim, or the stalk of a plant); *nui* (many). Many plant

Kākā: New Zealand parrot

stalks, or swimming or crossing a river.

Kākāpō Ground parrot.

Kākāpuaka *kākā* (parrot); *puaka* (dry twigs or flowers).

Kākaramea A contraction of kakara taramea. Scent made from gum extracted from the leaves of spear-grass. See Karamea.

Kākāriki Parakeet.

Kākātahi *kākā* (parrot); *tahi* (single). One parrot.

Kakepuku Correctly, and in full, Kakīpuku-o-Kahurere. *Kakī* (neck); *puku* (swollen). The name was given hundreds of years ago by Rakataura, partly after his wife Kahurere, and partly because of the shape of the hill near Te Awamutu. It is also said that the full name is Kakepuku-te-aroaro-o-Kahukeke.

Kakīroa *kakī* (neck); *roa* (long). The name of a Waitaha ancestor, or one of the crew of the Ārai-te-uru canoe.

Kā-kōhaka-ruru-whenua In standard Māori the name would appear as Ngā-kōhanga-ruru-whenua. *Ngā* (the); *kōhanga* (nest); *ruru-whenua* (large owl, or morepork). The nests of the large owls. Some southern Māori digging for gold in the 1860s cooked and ate these owls, giving this name to what later became known as Moonlight Gully.

Kāmahi A native tree.

Kāmaka Rock or stone.

Kamautūrua The fastening of two bundles. The name of a chief of the Ārai-te-uru canoe was given to the Burnett Range.

Kamo To bubble up. Descriptive of the hot springs.

Kamokamo Winking. When the chief Porourangi was murdered, winking was adopted as a signal for the attack.

Kanapa Shining.

Kaniere The act of sawing greenstone.

Kanohi Eye, or face.

Kā-pākihi-whakatekateka-a-Waitaha *kā* (the); *pākihi* (open grass country); *whakatekateka* (to play with a dart); *a* (of); *Waitaha* (a tribe). The open grass country where the Waitaha people would have room to play the game of throwing darts. It is a very old name for the Canterbury Plains, and there is an inference that there was no room for such sport in the hills and gullies of Otago.

Kaparatehau *Ka para* (to sport); *te* (the); *hau* (wind). The wind is sporting. The name probably comes from the chief Te Hau, who was offended by Kupe, who caused the area to be inundated by the sea. It is the shallow lake or lagoon that later received the name Lake Grassmere.

Kāpiti Short for Ko-te-waewae-kāpiti-o-Tara-raua-ko-Rangitāne, the place where the boundaries of Tara and Rangitāne divide.

Kaponga A tree-fern.

Kā-poupou-o-te-Rakihouia The posts of Rakihouia, the son of Rākaihaitū, who dug the southern lakes. Rakihouia made a number of eel weirs, and this very old name for the Canterbury coast was given because of the posts he planted in the rivers in order to make eel-weirs.

Kapowairua *kapo* (snatching);

wairua (soul). A place in Tom Bowling Bay where demons snatch at the spirits of the dead as they pass to the afterlife.

Kapuarangi *kapua* (cloud); *rangi* (sky). Cloudy sky.

Kāpuka A native tree.

Kapuka-tau-mohaka Snaring pigeons with a string. A name that describes pigeon-hunting on the slopes of Mount Cargill.

Kā-puke-māeroero *kā*, or *ngā* (the); *puke* (hill); *māeroero* (wild men of the hills). The hills of the wild men. This was the Māori name for the foothills of the Southern Alps.

Kapuni An assembly. A place named by Turi of the Aotea canoe where he and his men camped by a river.

Karaka A native tree.

Karamea A shortened form of kakara taramea. *Kakara* (scent); *taramea* (spear-grass). The scent was made from the gum extracted from the leaves of the spear-grass. The kakara taramea made by the women of the Karamea district was highly valued, and Māori travelled long distances to barter food and greenstone for it.

Karamū A native shrub.

Karangahake *karanga* to welcome); *hake* (hunchback). Loosely translated as a Meeting of the hunchbacks, a phrase that describes the cluster of low hills in the vicinity.

Karangahape A shellfish. There is a story that a hill on the East Coast was called Karanga-a-Hape, because the chief Hape pursued a wounded moa up a hillside. He attacked it with his taiaha (weapon), but it kicked him, his leg was broken, and he rolled down the hill.

Karangarua *karanga* (to call); *rua* (two). This is a term for someone who is doubly related to someone else, i.e., through two lines.

Karāpiro *karā* (stone); *piro* (stinking).

Karapiti To fasten, or place side by side.

Karatia Māori form of Galatia, a missionary settlement on the Whanganui River, originally called Hikurangi.

Karekare Surf.

Kāretu Sweet-scented grass.

Karioi To loiter. A place where the Māori sometimes lingered.

Kāriri Māori form of Galilee. Early mission station.

Karitāne *kari* (to dig); *tāne* (men). Men digging. This may be a reference to the digging of a ditch to catch eels. Another explanation is that while the Huriawa pā was being besieged, some of the men slipped out on a fishing expedition leaving only the wounded (kari) to defend the pā.

Karori In full, Te-kaha-o-ngā-rore, The rope of the snares. Before European settlement the Karori valley was noted for its birds.

Karoro Seagull. The proper name may be Kararoa. *Kara* (beach); *roa* (long). Long shelving beach.

Kartigi Correctly, Kātiki. *Kā*, or *ngā* (the); *tiki* (carved figure). The tiki.

Karumoerangi To day-dream.

Katikati Nibbling. In full, Katikati-o-Tamatekapua, The nibbling of Tamatekapua. When they reached this place, Tamatekapua's men ate their food quickly, but the captain of the Arawa canoe kept nibbling his, hence the name.

Katipō A small venomous spider.

Kauaeranga No crossing here.

Kauana Māori form of the name Cowan, who was an early settler in the Ōreti River basin.

Kauarapaoa *kau* (to swim); *ara* (path); *Paoa* (or *Pawa*). The route by which Pawa swam across the river. Pawa was Kupe's servant. He went up the Whanganui River, and swam to the other side to get some kōrau (native turnip) and was drowned. This was an important place because here Kupe heard voices. They were the voices of the weka, kōkako, and tīwaiwaka. When he found they were birds and not men, he returned to the mouth of the river.

Kaukapakapa *kau* (to swim); *kapakapa* (flapping). To swim with much splashing. There were wild ducks in the creek, and they were chased away or hunted with much flapping of their wings.

Kaukau Corrupt form of Kākā, parrot.

Kauri tree

Kaungaroa Correctly, Kauangaroa. *Kauanga* (ford); *roa* (long). Long ford.

Kauri Short for Kauri-hohore, a bald or smooth-barrelled kauri tree.

Kauroa *kau* (to swim); *roa* (long). To swim for a long time.

Kauwaewhakatoro *kauwae* (jaw); *whakatoro* (to stretch out). The Ngāi Tahu tribe, fighting against Ngāti Māmoe, sent out decoys at Hillend. Then they closed round their victims like jaws round food.

Kawakawa A native tree. Kawakawa at East Cape is in full Te Kawakawa-mai-tawhiti, and has come from Hawaiki.

Kawarau *kawa* (shrub); *rau* (many). Many shrubs.

Kawatiri There are many explanations of the meaning of the Māori name for the Buller River, some of which are lengthy. A noted authority believed that it should really have been Ko Awatere, The swift river.

Kawau Shag.

Kawerau *kawe* (to carry); *rau* (many). Many carriers. The district was first settled by the Tini-o-Kawerau tribe from Hawaiki, which took its name from a chief.

Kāwhia In full, Ka-awhia. The name was given by Turi of the Aotea canoe when he entered the harbour. An awhiawhi was a ceremony performed on entering a new land to protect the explorers from evil influences. Each phrase of the karakia (chant) that Turi used began with ka.

Kawiti The Māori chief who fought against the British forces in the Bay of Islands.

Kēkerengū The name comes from a young Māori chief who had to flee to this place because of the enmity of Rangihaeata.

Kenana Māori form of Canaan.

Kenepuru Sandy silt.

Kerepehi Clod of earth. An old Māori said that it was a clod of earth 'easy to hold'.

Kerikeri To keep on digging.

Keteketerau *ketekete* (to click the tongue); *rau* (many). Many clickings of the tongue. Tara, son of Whātonga, set out to avenge the killing of his dog. He landed at what was then the outlet of the Ahuriri lagoon, Napier, and jumped ashore. Then he remembered he had left his pūtātara (trumpet) at Wairoa, and gave vent to his surprise by many clickings of his tongue.

Kete: basket

Ketemarae *kete* (basket); *marae* (courtyard). Basket on the marae. An old woman at the pā on the site of Normanby had only one basket of food to give to visitors. She put it on the marae.

Ketetahi *kete* (basket); *tahi* (one). One basket.

Kiekie A native vine.

Kihikihi Cicada. An onomatopoeic name.

Kikowhakarere *kiko* (body); *whakarere* (cast away). Bodies cast away. The Māori of Whangapoua surprised those at Kikowhakarere, but were defeated. They had to leave many behind who were dead or wounded, and from this the place received its name.

Kilmog A whaler's pronunciation of *kirimoko* (a species of mānuka, or tea-tree). It was used to make an infusion of tea.

Kimiākau *kimi* (to look for); *ākau* (coast). To look for the coast. A band of explorers followed the course of the Arrow River to see if they could find a way through to the West Coast.

Kimihia To seek.

Kinohaku *kino* (bad, or ugly); *haku* (kingfish).

Kiokio A native fern.

Kiore Native rat.

Kioreroa *kiore* (rat); *roa* (long). Long rat.

Kirikau *kiri* (skin); *kau* (bare). Naked. A battle in which the contestants were naked was fought here long ago.

Kirikiri-katata *kirikiri* (a mass of rock); *katata* (sharp points). A sharp-pointed mass of rock. The Māori name for the Mount Cook Range.

Kirikiriroa *kirikiri* (gravel); *roa* (long). Long stretches of gravel. The Māori name for Hamilton.

Kirikōpuni Dark-skinned eel.

Kiri-o-Hinekai The skin of Hinekai. It was a hot pool at Rotorua that was useful in the cure of skin diseases.

Kiripaka Quartz, or flint.

Kiritaki To pull off the bark. There was a tōtara tree from which a great deal of bark was taken.

Kiwi Native flightless bird.
Kiwitahi *kiwi* (bird); *tahi* (one). Single kiwi.
Kiwitea *kiwi* (bird); *tea* (white). White kiwi.
Kōhai A form of *kōwhai* (flowering tree).
Kōhanga Nest.
Kohekohe A native tree.
Kohi Seasick. When the Mataatua canoe paddled towards the shore in the Bay of Plenty, the groundswell made Wairaka, the daughter of Toroa, sick.
Kohimārama *kohi* (point); *mārama* (light). Light on a headland.
Kōhuaora Cooked in an earth oven while alive. It refers to an event of long ago at Papatoetoe.
Kohukete *kohu* (mist); *kete* (basket). Mist in the form of a basket. The chief Koha took this form of mist as the sign of an approaching enemy.
Kohukohu Moss, seaweed, a plant, or a tree.
Kohumaru *kohu* (mist); *maru* (sheltered). Sheltered from the fog.
Kohunui *kohu* (mist); *nui* (big). Big mist, or ground mist.
Kōhuratahi *kōhura* (to sprout); *tahi* (single). May refer to a *kō* (digging stick).

Kohutai *kohu* (mist); *tai* (tide). Sea foam.
Kōiro Conger eel.
Kōkako Native crow.
Kōkakoriki *kōkako* (crow); *riki* (little, or few). Few kokako.
Kōkiri To dash forward, or charge.
Kokonga Angle or corner. The name probably comes from the bend in the river.
Kōkopu Small freshwater fish.
Kokori A small bay.
Kōkōwai Red earth, from which red ochre was obtained by burning.
Kōmata End of a range of hills.
Kōnini Fruit of native fuchsia.
Kongahu Boulders. There are many boulders in this part of the Buller district.

Kō: digging implement

Kōpaki To wrap.

Kopi-o-kaitangata *kopi* (gorge); *o* (of); *kaitangata* (man-eater). Cannibal gorge. Parties of Māori travelled to the west coast through this gorge, their passage being marked by cannibal feasts. An alternative name is Kai-pai-o-kaitangata, Good feed of human flesh.

Kōpū Belly.

Kōpua Deep pool.

Kōpuarahi *kōpua* (deep pool); *rahi* (large). Large deep pool.

Kōpuaranga *kōpua* (deep pool); *ranga* (shoal of fish). Fish in a deep pool.

Kōpuawhara *kōpua* (deep pool); *whara* (plant). Deep pool with astelia growing round it.

Kōpuku Closely woven cloak.

Kōpūriki *kōpū* (belly); *riki* (little). Little stomach.

Kōpuku: cloak

Kōpūreherehe *kōpū* (belly); *reherehe* (wrinkled). The name refers to eels that had been fat, but had become shrunk and wrinkled.

Kopuriki *kopu* (small fish); *riki* (few). Hardly any fish.

Kopūtai High tide. Some Māori landed at Port Chalmers and went soundly to sleep. When they woke they found that their canoes had drifted away on the tide. They shouted 'Kopūtai!' (High tide!)

Kōputaroa *kōputa* (snare for catching parakeets); *roa* (long). Long snare.

Koputauaki To relax comfortably after a feast, which was exactly what happened after a cannibal banquet.

Koputīraha Lying back with the arms above the head. An attitude adopted by a chief at this place, which is now the business centre of Nelson.

Kōrakonui *kōrako* (albino); *nui* (big). Big albino.

Koranui Short for Korokoronui. *Korokoro* (throat); *nui* (big). Big throat. The valley is long and narrow and may be said to resemble a throat.

Koreke Quail.

Kōrere Channel.

Koriniti Māori form of Corinth.

A missionary settlement on the Whanganui River.
Kōrito Unexpanded leaves, or a variety of greenstone.
Korokata Māori form of Golgotha. Te Rauparaha raided this place, just outside Whanganui, and 14 years later the Reverend Richard Taylor was so horrified by the number of human bones in evidence that he called the place Golgotha.
Korokoro Throat.
Koromiko Native veronica.
Kororāreka *kororā* (blue penguin); *reka* (sweet, or tasty). An old chief lay dying and expressed a wish for a penguin. After much searching one was found. When it was cooked he was too weak to eat it, but he drank some of the water in which it had been boiled, and murmured, 'Ka reka te kororā!' (How sweet is the penguin!)
Koru To fold, or folded.
Ko-te-kete-ika-a-Tutekawa
The fish basket of Tutekawa. A proverb that applied to Lakes Forsyth and Ellesmere because they were so full of fish.
Kotemaori Incorrect form of Ko te moari, the giant swing.
Kotinga Boundary line.

Kōtuku White heron. It is an abbreviation of the Māori name for Lake Brunner, Kōtuku-whakaoka. *Whakaoka* (to stab). The reference is to the kōtuku darting its long, sharp beak down to catch fish. Another name for Lake Brunner is Kōtuku-moana.
Koukourarata Tame owl. Māori name for Port Levy.
Kōura Crayfish.
Kōurariki Whale-feed. Māori name for Cape Providence.
Koutu Promontory. A descriptive name.
Kōwai Shortened form of Kōwhai (flowering tree).
Kōwhai Flowering tree.
Kōwhatu Stone.
Kūaotuna *kūao* (young); *tuna* (eel). Young of eels.
Kuirau *kui* (old woman); *rau* (many). A picnic spot at Rotorua where the old women cooked the kai (food).
Kūmara Sweet potato. Kūmara on the West Coast, however, was named after a flower, either of the convolvulus, or the bush-lawyer. It may originally have been kohimara.
Kumeroa *kume* (to pull); *roa* (long). A long pull.
Kumeū *kume* (to pull); *ū* (breast).

Pulling the breasts. An action undertaken by women to incite a war party.

Kupenga-a-Kupe *kupenga* (net); *a* (of); *Kupe* (the famous explorer). Kupe left a net here at Jackson's Head as a sign of his visit.

Kurīpuni *kurī* (native dog); *puni* (place of encampment).

Kurīwao *kurī* (dog); *wao* (bush). Wild dog.

Kurow Correctly, Kohurau. *Kohu* (mist); *rau* (many). Many fogs. The name probably came originally from one of the crew of the Ārai-te-uru.

Kūwhā-rua-o-Kahu As Kahu-mata-momoe went ashore at Lake Rotoiti, he threw off his clothes. His grandsons laughed and shouted 'Ho! Ho! There go Kahu's legs!' and so the place was named.

Mahau: porch, shelter

M

Māeneene Smooth.

Maerewhenua Possibly this should be Maerowhenua. *Maero* (original inhabitants); *whenua* (land). Land of the wild men, or strange folk. An alternative meaning and spelling could be Maruwhenua; *maru* (shelter). The name is applied to the rock shelters with unusual Māori paintings near Duntroon.

Maero Wild men.

Māhaki Mild, or calm.

Māhakipawa *māhaki* (calm); *pawa* (smoke). When Te Rauparaha raided the valley, the inhabitants saw him coming and set fire to their pā. Te Rauparaha saw the smoke rising calmly in the air, and said, 'I see smoke!'

Mahana Warm.

Māharahara To remember another's fault.

Mahau Porch, shelter.

Maheno Island. The name was conferred by a Pākehā.

Māhēpuku A rounded sinker. The Māori name for Pepin Island.

Māhia To sound, or resound. The Māhia Peninsula was named Te Māhia-mai-tawhiti after a place in Tahiti.

Māhinahina Refers to grey hair.

Māhinapua *Māhina* (proper name); *pua* (flower). Māhina's flower.

Mahitahi Correctly, Maitahi. *Mai* (garment); *tahi* (one). Single garment.

Māhoe A native tree.

Māhoenui *māhoe* (tree); *nui* (big, or plenty of). Many māhoe trees.

Māhoetahi *māhoe* (tree); *tahi* (single). Single māhoe tree.

Māhunui The name of the canoe in which Māui came to New Zealand. This canoe was the South Island, Te Waka-a-Māui, from which he fished up (discovered) Te Ika-a-Māui, the North Island. Also Maahunui.

Mahurangi One of the explanations of the name is that the Tainui canoe called in here before the portage over the Tāmaki Isthmus, and that this place, later known as Warkworth, was so-called after the chieftainess who designed the Tainui canoe in Hawaiki.

Mahuta Named after the third Māori King, son of Tāwhiao.

Māia Brave.

Maiki The high place. The peak where the flagstaff stands at Russell.

Maimai The place in Westland is not a Māori word, but comes from a corruption of the Australian word for a rough camp or bivouac, brought over by the gold-diggers.

Mairangi Shortened form of Ōmairangi, the place of Mairangi.

Mairekura *maire* (native tree); *kura* (red garment). Red garment hanging on a maire tree. A chief dared his enemies to cross the Whanganui River by hanging his red garment in a tree.

Māīroa *māī* (preserved mussels out of their shells); *roa* (many).

Maitai The proper spelling is Maitahi, and refers to one particular mataī or mai (black pine) that grew on the bank of the river.

Mākāhu *mā* (white); *kāhu* (hawk). White hawk.

Mākara Head, or **Makara**, to come or go.

Mākaraka *mā* (short for *manga*; stream); *karaka* (native tree). A place where karaka trees grew by a stream.

Makarau *maka* (to throw); *rau* (to catch in a net).

Mākāretu *mā* (stream); *kāretu* (sweet-scented grass). Stream where the sweet-scented grass grows.

Makarewa *maka* (fish-hook); *rewa* (floating). Fish-hooks floating on the water. After baiting hooks to catch eels, the local Māori found them floating on the surface of the water after a storm.

Mākarini Named for Sir Donald McLean.

Makarora *maka* (South Island form of *manga*: stream); *rora* (spread out).

Makarore *maka* (part of a bird-snare); *rore* (to ensnare).

Mākatote *mā* (stream); *katote* (tree-fern). Tree-ferns growing by a stream.

Mākauri *mā* (stream); *kauri* (native tree). Kauri growing by a stream.

Makawhio *maka* (South Island form of *manga*; stream); *whio* (blue duck). Stream of the blue duck.

Makerōnia Māori form of Macedonia. The pā was built at the time of the Hauhau wars.

Mākerikeri *mā* (stream); *kerikeri* (rushing violently). Turbulent stream.

Maketū Named after a place in Hawaiki.

Mākiekie *mā* (stream); *kiekie* (native flower plant). Stream where the kiekie grows.

Mākikihi *mā* (stream); *kikihi* (cicada). Stream of the cicadas. Or kikihi may refer to the sound of the cicadas, in which case the meaning is Murmuring stream.

Mākino *mā* (stream); *kino* (bad).

Mākirikiri *mā* (stream); *kirikiri* (gravelly). Gravelly stream.

Mākōhine *mā* (stream); *kōhine* (girl). Girl's stream.

Mākōtuku *mā* (stream); *kōtuku* (white heron). Stream of the white heron. Alternatively, *kōtuku* could be *kōtukutuku* (fuchsia).

Mākōura *mā* (stream); *kōura* (freshwater crayfish). Crayfish stream.

Mākōwhai *mā* (stream); *kōwhai*

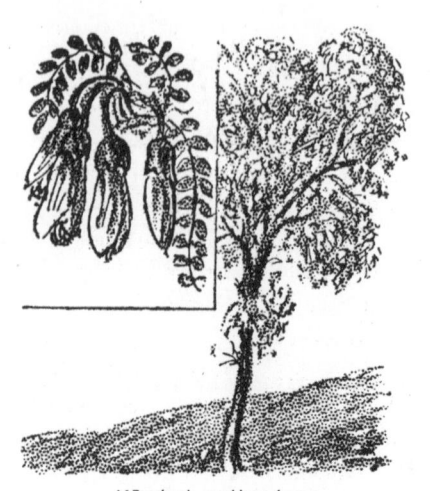

Kōwhai: native tree

(native tree). Kōwhai stream. A name given by a Pākehā.
Mākū   Wet.
Mākurī   *mā* (stream); *kurī* (dog). Dog creek.
Mamaku   Tree-fern.
Mana   Power. Mana Island near Wellington is, in full, Te Mana-o-Kupe-ki-Aotearoa, the ability of Kupe to cross the ocean to Aotearoa. Kupe's daughter suggested that the name be given to the island.
Manaia   A carved Māori figure with beak. Manaia in Taranaki was named after a local Māori chief. Manaia on the south side of Whāngārei Harbour was named after a chief who climbed the hill. When at the summit he quarrelled with his wife and kicked her and his slave, and the whole family were turned into stones by the gods.
Manakau   *mana* (authority or prestige); *kau* (alone). Prestige alone. Te Rauparaha subdued the local inhabitants by means of his prestige without having to resort to war.
Manapōuri   Short for manawa-popore. *Manawa* (heart); *popore* (throbbing). Anxious heart. A name given by a traveller whose canoe was threatened by a storm. The true name of the lake is Moturau, meaning Many islands.
Manaroa   *mana* (power); *roa* (long).
Manawaora   *manawa* (heart); *ora* (healthy).
Manawarū   Anxious, apprehensive, or enraptured.
Manawatahi   Out of breath. The name of the Three Kings Islands. The chief Raura owned one of them and swam across from the mainland, arriving exhausted on the shore of the island.
Manawatū   *manawa* (heart); *tū* (to stand). Heart standing still with fear, or depressed spirit. Haunui was pursuing his wife, and when he came to the river he held his hand to his heart and gave it the name Manawatū.
Māniatoto   The name in full is Mānia-o-toto. *Mānia* (plain); *o* (of); *toto* (blood). It was the scene of many bloody battles.
Māniatutu   *mānia* (plain); *tutu* (tree). Plain where the tutu grows.
Manuherekia   *manu* (bird); *herekia* (tied). The tied bird. A Māori scout tied a wounded kākā here to mark the crossing place.
Mānuka   Tea-tree.
Manukau   *manu* (bird); *kau* (to wade). Wading birds. The original

name of the Manukau Harbour was Te Mānukanuka-a-Hotunui, *te* (the); *mānukanuka* (anxiety); *o* (of); Hotunui (or Hoturoa), the captain of the Tainui canoe. Hotunui became anxious when encountering heavy breakers at the harbour entrance.

Manunui   Correctly, Mananui. *Mana* (prestige); *nui* (large). Great prestige. It refers to the power and prestige of the chief Pāpārangi.

Manupīrua   Two little birds.

Manurewa   *manu* (kite); *rewa* (floating). Floating kite. A kite once broke loose at Ōnehunga and floated over Manurewa.

Manutahi   *manu* (bird); *tahi* (single). Solitary bird.

Manutītī   *manu* (bird); *tītī* (mutton bird). The small island in Dusky Sound was so named because there was a colony of birds there, and Māori could always collect a few in the autumn.

Manutuke   *manu* (bird); *tuke* (elbow, or to twitch).

Manuwhaea   *manu* (bird); *whaea* (split). The split bird.

Manga-a-te-tipua   *manga* (stream); *a* (of); *te* (the); *tipua* (demon). Goblin creek, a suitable name for the boiling stream at Ketetahi.

Mangahao   Short for Manga-a-hao. *Manga* (stream); *a* (of); *hao* (netting). Stream where cockabullies are caught.

Mangaharakeke   *manga* (stream); *harakeke* (flax). Flax creek.

Mangahoe   *manga* (stream); *hoe* (to paddle). Paddling in the stream.

Mangahuia   *manga* (stream); *huia* (extinct bird). Huia stream.

Mangaiti   *manga* (stream); *iti* (small). Little stream.

Mangakāhia   *manga* (stream); *kāhia*, or *kōhia* (passion vine). Passion vine stream.

Mangakaiwhiria   *manga* (stream); *kaiwhiria* (climbing plant).

Mangakino   *manga* (stream); *kino* (bad). Useless stream.

Mangakura   *manga* (stream); *kura* (red, or red ochre). Red stream.

Mangamāhoe   *manga* (stream); *māhoe* (whitewood tree). Māhoe stream.

Mangamāhū   *manga* (stream); *māhū* (gentle). Gently flowing stream.

Mangamaire   *manga* (stream); *maire* (tree, New Zealand olive). Maire stream.

Mangamako   Probably short for Mangamakomako. *Manga* (stream); *makomako* (wineberry tree). Wineberry stream.

Mangamate *manga* (stream); *mate* (death). Stream of death.

Mangāmāunu *mangā* (barracouta fish); *māunu* (bait). Barracouta bait.

Mangamingi Probably Mangamingimingi in full. *Manga* (stream); *mingimingi* (shrub). Mingimingi stream.

Mangamuka *manga* (stream); *muka* (shoot of nīkau). Nīkau palm stream.

Nīkau: New Zealand palm

Mangamutu *manga* (stream); *mutu* (finished). Dead-end stream.

Mangangārara *manga* (stream); *ngārara* (lizard). Lizard stream.

Māngangūkaiota *mānga* (scraps); *ngū* (eat greedily); *kaiota* (raw). I will eat you raw. Said by one chief to another if he dared to cross a line between them. The chief did so, and was eaten raw.

Manganui *manga* (stream); *nui* (big). Big stream.

Manganui-a-te-ao *manga* (stream); *nui* (big); *a* (of); *te* (the); *ao* (world). The great stream of the land. It is famous in legend, and has two other names equally grand: The powerful and famous river of Rongomai, and The river of ever-dancing waters and steep, echoing cliffs.

Manga-o-Hae *manga* (stream); *o* (of); *Hae* (proper name). The stream of Hae.

Manga-o-Hutu *manga* (stream); *o* (of); *Hutu* (proper name). The stream of Hutu.

Mangaone *manga* (stream); *one* (beach). Sandy stream.

Manga-o-Noho *manga* (stream); *o* (of); *Noho* (proper name). Noho's stream.

Mangaoranga Correctly, Manga-o-Rongomai. *Manga* (stream); *o* (of); *Rongomai* (a god). Stream of Rongomai.

Manga-o-Taki *manga* (stream); *o* (of); *Taki* (proper name). Taki's stream.

Manga-o-Wera *manga* (stream); *o* (of); *Wera* (proper name). Wera's stream.

Mangapai *manga* (stream); *pai* (good). Stream of good water.

Mangapākehā The correct name is Mangapākia. *Manga* (stream); *pākia* (to be touched).

Mangapākihi *manga* (stream); *pākihi* (open grass country). Stream through open country.

Mangapapa *manga* (stream); *papa* (flat country). Stream through flat country.

Mangapēhi *manga* (stream); *pēhi* (sticks for making fire, or trouble). Stream of trouble.

Mangapiko *manga* (stream); *piko* (bent). Crooked stream.

Mangapiri *manga* (stream); *piri* (to hide, or native burr). Hidden stream.

Mangapōuri *manga* (stream); *pōuri* (dark). Dark stream.

Mangapuaka *manga* (stream); *puaka* (bird-snare). Stream of the bird-snare.

Mangapūrua *manga* (stream); *pūrua* (abundant, or plenty). Stream of plenty.

Mangarākau *manga* (stream); *rākau* (tree or timber). Stream by the trees.

Mangaramarama *manga* (stream); *ramarama* (myrtle tree).

Mangarātā *manga* (stream); *rātā* (tree). Rātā stream.

Mangarawa *manga* (stream); *rawa* (swamp). Swampy stream.

Mangarengarenga *manga* (stream); *rengarenga* (renga-lily). Stream of lilies.

Mangareporepo *manga* (stream); *reporepo* (soft mud). Muddy creek.

Mangarimu *manga* (stream); *rimu* (tree). Rimu stream.

Mangaroa *manga* (stream); *roa* (long). Long stream.

Mangarōhutu *manga* (stream); *rōhutu* (myrtle). Myrtle stream.

Mangarua *manga* (stream); *rua* (two). Two streams.

Mangatainoka *manga* (stream); *tainoka* (native broom). Broom stream.

Mangatangi *manga* (stream); *tangi* (weeping). Babbling brook.

Mangatapu *manga* (stream); *tapu* (sacred). Forbidden stream.

Mangatarata *manga* (stream); *tarata* (tree). Tarata stream.

Mangatāwhiri *manga* (stream); *tāwhiri* (tree). Stream where the tāwhiri grows.

Mangatea *manga* (stream); *tea* (clear, or white). Clear stream.

Mangaterā *manga* (stream); *te* (the); *rā* (sun). Sunny stream.

Mangatere *manga* (stream); *tere* (to flow). Flowing stream.

Mangateretere *manga* (stream); *teretere* (swiftly flowing). Swift-flowing stream.

Mangatina *manga* (stream); *tina* (exhausted). The first Māori to reach the stream were exhausted by the effort of crossing.

Mangatini *manga* (stream); *tini* (many). Stream with many branches. The country this stream in the Buller district flows through is very broken.

Mangatītī *manga* (stream); *tītī* (mutton bird). Stream of the mutton birds.

Mangatoetoe *manga* (stream); *toetoe* (plume grass). Toetoe stream.

Mangatoki *manga* (stream); *toki* (adze). But possibly a contraction of Mangatītoki: *manga* (stream); *tītoki* (tree). Tītoki stream.

Māngatu *mā* (stream); *ngatu* (part of the raupō). Stream of the reeds.

Mangawai *manga* (stream); *wai* (water).

Mangawara *manga* (stream); *wara* (indistinct sound).

Mangaweka *manga* (stream); *weka* (wood-hen). Creek of the wood-hens.

Mangawhai *manga* (stream); *Whai* (name of a chief). River of Te Whai. Te Whai fled from Ngāpuhi and settled on the headland where the rivers meet.

Mangawharariki *manga* (stream); *wharariki* (a kind of flax). Stream where the flax grows.

Mangawharawhara *manga* (stream); *wharawhara* (perching lily). Wharawhara stream.

Mangawhare *manga* (stream); *whare* (house). Stream by the house.

Mangawhata *manga* (stream); *whata* (raised storehouse). Stream by the storehouse.

Mangawhero *manga* (stream); *whero* (red). Red stream.

Māngere Lazy. When Īhenga crossed the Waikato, he came to this place and rested while his young men prepared food. They took so long that he was angry, and named the place Laziness.

Mangōnui *mangō* (shark); *nui* (big). Large shark.

Weka: wood-hen

Mangōparerua Two hammerhead sharks.
Mangōrei *mangō* (shark); *rei* (tooth). Shark's tooth.
Mangungu Closely knit, or woven.
Māori People, indigenous New Zealanders. When the word enters into a name, as in Māori Hill or Māori Creek, it is safe to say that it has been conferred by a Pākehā.
Māpere To fly.
Māpiu In full, Māpiupiu. *Mā* (stream); *piupiu* (fern). Ferny creek.
Māpou Native tree.
Māpourika The word is unknown. It may possibly be a South Island form of Māpouriki.
Māpouriki *māpou* (tree); *riki* (little). The small māpou trees.
Māpua Bearing an abundance of fruit.
Maraekākaho *marae* (village assembly ground); *kākaho* (plumes of the toetoe). The courtyard surrounded by plume grass.
Maraekura *marae* (courtyard); *kura* (man of prowess). When Turi reached the Kaupokonui River his enchanted cloak opened twice and spread out, and he called the place Maraekura.

Marae: meeting ground

Maraeroa *marae* (courtyard); *roa* (long). Long courtyard.
Maraetai *marae* (open space); *tai* (coast). Open space by the seashore.
Maraeweka *marae* (meeting ground); *weka* (wood-hen). Weka on the marae.
Mārahau *māra* (garden); *hau* (wind). Windy garden.
Marakeke Probably Mārakerake (bald).
Marama Moon.
Maramarua *marama* (month); *rua* (two). Two months.
Marangai East wind. Also means North wind.
Maranui The name in full should be Maraenui. *Marae* (expanse); *nui* (big). Great expanse. It refers

Māraroa

to the expanse of ocean visible from Lyall Bay.

Māraroa *māra* (cultivation); *roa* (long). Long cultivated area.

Mārarua *māra* (cultivation); *rua* (two). Two plantations.

Māra-whiu-pungarehu *māra* (cultivation); *whiu* (to throw); *pungarehu* (ashes). The cultivation overcast with ashes.

Mareretu *marere* (to let down); *retu* (part of a fishing net). To let down the net. The original name has been contracted.

Marewa Raised up, or light soil.

Marino Calm, or peaceful.

Māriri Unripe fruit of the tawa tree.

Marokopa *maro* (kilt), or *mārō* (stiff); *kopa* (to fold, or lame). The place where Turi of the Aotea canoe folded his girdle, or where he became lame.

Maromākū *maro* (girdle); *mākū* (wet). Wet kilt.

Maropiu *maro* (kilt); *piu* (to swing). Kilt waving in the breeze.

Marotiri *maro* (apron); *tiri* (to throw or place beside). Placed beside the apron.

Mārua Valley.

Māruakoa *mārua* (valley); *koa* (glad). Happy valley.

Mātakitaki

Maruia Sheltered, like a valley deep in the hills.

Matā Quartz or flint.

Matahara *mata* (face); *hara* (ugly). Ugly face.

Matahiwi *mata* (face); *hiwi* (ridge). The ridge above the cliff.

Matahorua *mata* (face, or eye); *horua* (sobbing). Weeping.

Mātai Sea, or **Mataī**, a native tree.

Mataīhuka Black pine.

Mataīnui *mataī* (black pine); *nui* (big, or many). Plenty of black pine.

Mātairangi An observation post on a hill, so named because of its commanding position on Te Ahumairangi (Tinakori Hill).

Mātaitakiara *mātai* (look-out point); *takiara* (bright morning star). The look-out point from which the morning star can be seen.

Mātaiwhetū *mātai* (to look at); *whetū* (star). To gaze at the stars.

Matakana Distrustful, or wary.

Matakānui *mata* (face); *kā* (blow, or scar); *nui* (big). The scarred face of a big cliff.

Matakinokino *mata* (face); *kinokino* (ugly). Ill-favoured face.

Mātakitaki To gaze at. The name

was given to a number of places that Kupe and others inspected when they first came to New Zealand.

Matakohe *mata* (headland); *kohe* short for *kohekohe* (a tree). Pinnacle of land where kohekohe trees grow.

Matamata Point, or extremity. The point of land on which the pā (fortified village) was built projected like a tongue into the surrounding swamp.

Matamau Stingy. Or *mātā* (heap); *mau* (products of the soil). Heap of vegetables.

Matanehunehu *mata* (headland); *nehunehu* (spray). A headland drenched with flying spray. In a stiff northerly the spray flies right over the cliff.

Matangi Breeze.

Matangirau *matangi* (breeze); *rau* (leaf). Wind among the leaves.

Matanuku *mata* (cliff); *nuku* (to move or extend). Named by Kahumatamomoe when he came to a cliff where there was a stone projecting from the face.

Matapehi-o-te-rangi The first streak of dawn from the heavens. Māori name for McLaren's Peak, Nelson.

Matapīa *mata* (headland); *pīa* (to bathe with water). Headland washed by the sea.

Matapōuri Gloomy, a black teal, or a shellfish.

Mātapu To make clear of tapu. There was a prolific miro tree at this place, which attracted flocks of pigeons. An old chief made it tapu or sacred to himself so that all the pigeons would be his. No doubt it became necessary to clear the tree of tapu at a later date if others were to have a share of the pigeons.

Mātārae A headland.

Matarau A number of points, used in describing a rocky shore.

Matarawa *mata* (headland); *rawa* (numerous). Many headlands.

Matariki The Pleiades, or the north-east sea-breeze.

Mataroa *mata* (headland); *roa* (long). Long headland.

Matau: fish-hook

Matata Dividing waters.
Matatapu *mata* (headland); *tapu* (sacred). Sacred headland.
Matātoki *matā* (flint); *toki* (adze). Flint adze.
Matau Fish-hook. At one place this name was given to a river that has a bend resembling a fish-hook, to another where there is a beach of the same shape. Matau, the original name for the Clutha River, was properly Mata-au, a current or eddy in an expanse of water.
Matauira *mata* (point of land); *uira* (lightning, or gleaming).
Mataura Reddish, eddying water. The swamp water that drains into the river is impregnated with oxide of iron.
Mātauri *mā* (stream); *tauri* (ornament of feathers).
Mātāwai Fountainhead, or source of a spring.
Matawhāura Warfare, or battle.
Matawhero *mata* (face); *whero* (red). Red face.
Matiaha After Matiaha Tiramōrehu. A form of Matthias.
Mātīere *mā* (stream); *tīere* (scent). Scented stream.
Matiu Somes Island in Wellington Harbour was named after Matiu, the daughter of Kupe.
Mātukituki *mā* (stream); *tukituki* (dashing). The dashing or pounding stream. The Mātukituki River was probably named after a chief.
Matuku Bittern, or blue heron.

Matuku: bittern

Mauku Small ground ferns.
Maungaatua *maunga* (mountain); *atua* (god). Mountain of the gods.
Maungaharuru *maunga* (mountain); *haruru* (rumbling). Rumbling mountain. When the Tākitimu canoe was travelling down the east coast on its way to search for greenstone, a high inland range was seen. The tohunga (priest) took a piece of wood, which received life and flew to the top of the range in the shape of a bird. The mountain gave forth a rumbling sound.

Maungahaumi *maunga* (mountain); *haumi* (piece of wood used to lengthen a canoe). When at Whakatāne, Pawa the captain sent a party of men ashore to get a suitable piece of timber for a topside plank for the canoe, and they found it on this mountain.

Maungahuka *maunga* (mountain); *huka* (snow). Snowy mountain. This peak in the Tararua Range was usually snow-covered.

Maungahura *maunga* (mountain); *hura* (bare). Bald mountain.

Maungakaramea *maunga* (mountain); *karamea* (red ochre). There are many colours in the mountain, which is known to Pākehā as Rainbow Mountain.

Maungakiekie *maunga* (mountain); *kiekie* (plant). The mountain where the kiekie grows abundantly. It is the Māori name for One Tree Hill in Auckland.

Maunganamu *maunga* (mountain); *namu* (sandfly). Sandfly mountain.

Maunganui *maunga* (mountain); *nui* (big). Large mountain.

Maungapōhatu *maunga* (mountain); *pōhatu* (rock). Rocky mountain.

Maungaraki *maunga* (mountain); *raki* (north). Mountains running in a northerly direction.

Maungataniwha *maunga* (mountain); *taniwha* (monster). Taniwha mountain. The full Māori name for Mount Camel in Northland is Maunga-taniwha-whakarongo-rua, which has been translated as The taniwha that hears both east and west. The mountain is sacred to the Ngāpuhi tribe.

Maungatapere *maunga* (mountain); *tapere* (place for meeting). Meeting place of mountains.

Maungatapu *maunga* (mountain); *tapu* (sacred or forbidden). Forbidden mountain.

Maungatautari *maunga* (mountain); *tautari* (upright stick). Maungatautari was the ancient name for Cambridge.

Maungatī *maunga* (mountain); *tī* (cabbage-tree). Cabbage-tree mountain.

Maungatiki *maunga* (mountain); *tiki* (fungus). Mountain where the fungus grows.

Maungatua Correctly, Maungaatua. *Maunga* (mountain); *atua* (god or spirit). Mountain of the spirits.

Maungatūroto *maunga* (mountain); *tū* (to stand); *roto* (lake). Mountain standing in a lake. Several of the volcanic peaks in Northland are surrounded by swamps, which were originally lagoons.

Maungawera *maunga* (mountain); *wera* (hot, or burnt). Burnt mountain.

Maungawhau *maunga* (mountain); *whau* (native tree). Whau hill.

Māwaro *mā* (stream); *waro* (charcoal). Charcoal stream.

Mawhera Widespread, open. The Māori name for Greymouth. It refers to the broad mouth of the Grey River.

Mawheraiti Little Mawhera; a tributary of the Mawhera or Grey River.

Meremere Evening star.

Meretoto *mere* (greenstone club); *toto* (blood). Blood-drinking club. It is the Māori name for Ship Cove.

Mihamihanui *mihamiha* (to begin to grow); *nui* (large). A large patch of growing vegetation.

Mihiwaka *mihi* (to greet); *waka* (canoe). To greet the canoe. It is said that when the Mihiwaka tunnel was being constructed, a store was kept by Mrs Walker. The Māori labourers gave the Māori pronunciation to her name, and Mrs Walker became Mihiwaka.

Miki A ridge of hills. Named after a woman who was carried away by the māeroero, or wild men.

Mikimiki Surprised expression. It is said that the full name is Mimikitanga-o-te-mata-o-Ngatuere, The surprised look on the face of Ngatuere. The Wairarapa was being invaded by a force of Hauhau, who were met unexpectedly by the chief Ngatuere Tāwhirimātea Tāwhao, who had a surprised look on his face when he saw them.

Miko Young shoot of the nīkau palm.

Mimi Stream, or creek.

Mere: greenstone club

Mimihau Passing shower.

Mina To desire.

Minarapa *mina* (to desire); *rapa* (to seek for). To look for something earnestly desired. The stream on Mount Taranaki was named after the chief Minarapa (Amou), who accompanied Bell and Carrington when they climbed the mountain.

Mirowharerā *miro* (native tree); *whare* (house); *rā* (sun). The miro tree that shades the house from the sun. The name appears on early maps as Merofafara, and it has been suggested that it was a Māori attempt to pronounce Meadowbank, as there was a gum-diggers' settlement of that name in the locality at Waipoua Forest.

Mitimiti Shallow water.

Mititai *miti* (to lap); *tai* (the coast). To lap the coast. Insects flew so close to the water here that they seemed to lick it.

Moa Large, extinct, flightless bird. Most places such as Moa Flat, Moa Creek, Moa Point, etc. have been so named because of the large number of moa bones found in the vicinity.

Moana Ocean, or large lake.

Moana-a-Toi *moana* (ocean); *a* (of); *Toi* (the explorer). Often Te Moana-a-Toi; The sea of Toi. The Bay of Plenty coast.

Moanakōtuku *moana* (large lake); *kōtuku* (white heron). Lake of the white heron. Māori name for Lake Brunner, where kōtuku would often be seen.

Moana-nui-a-Kiwa *moana* (ocean); *nui* (big); *a* (of); *Kiwa* (an ocean god). Usually Te Moana-nui-a-Kiwa; The great ocean of Kiwa. The Pacific Ocean.

Moana-tāpokopoko-a-Tāwhaki *moana* (ocean); *tāpokopoko* (billowy); *a* (of); *Tāwhaki* (a deity). The Tasman Sea. Tāwhaki travelled the ocean in search of his wife Hāpai.

Moanataiari *moana* (ocean); *taiari* (dashing). The stormy ocean.

Moana-whenua-pōuri *moana* (ocean); *whenua* (land); *pōuri* (sad, or dark). Sombre sound, the Māori name for Edwardson Arm in Fiordland, notable because there was usually a cloud over it casting a dark shadow.

Moawhango *moa* (large, extinct bird); *whango* (hoarse). Wheezy moa. Whango may be a corruption of whanga (valley), thus giving Moa valley.

Moeawatea *moe* (to sleep); *awatea* (daylight). Sleeping in the daytime.

Moehau *moe* (to sleep); *hau* (wind). Windy sleeping place, or The wind resting. The name in full is Moehau-o-Tamatekapua. Tamatekapua, captain of the Arawa canoe, was buried at Cape Colville, and the name was given by his son Kahumatamomoe. Hau probably refers to the life essence, and the name means The sleeping sacredness of Tamatekapua.

Moengawahine *moenga* (bed); *wahine* (woman). Woman's bed.

Moerā *moe* (to sleep); *rā* (the sun). Sleeping in the sun.

Moeraki *moe* (to sleep); *raki* (South Island form of *rangi*: sky, or day). A place for sleep by day.

Moerangi *moe* (to sleep); *rangi* (sky). Sleepy sky.

Moerewa *moe* (to sleep); *rewa* (floating like a bird apparently asleep). To sleep on high.

Moeroa *moe* (to sleep); *roa* (long). Long sleep, or resting, or sleeping place.

Moetapu *moe* (to sleep); *tapu* (sacred). Sacred sleep.

Moetere *moe* (to sleep); *tere* (swift). Swift sleep. Named after Moetere, who died in a snowstorm here on the Huiarau Range.

Mōhaka *mō* (used for); *haka* (dance). Place used for a dance. The name was imported from Hawaiki.

Mōhakatino *mō* (used); *haka* (dance); *tino* (exact, precise). The river was named because Turi of the Aotea canoe departed in person (tino) after having slept at Mōkau.

Haka: war dance

Mōioio The little blue penguin.

Mōkai Captive.

Mōkau Sleeping place. Named by Turi because he slept there.

Mōkauiti Little Mōkau.

Mōkihinui *mōkihi* (raft of dry flax stalks); *nui* (big). Large raft.

Mokohīnau *moko* (lizard); *hīnau* (native tree).

Mokoia Tattooed. On Mokoia Island, Lake Rotorua, a chief was fatally stabbed over the

Mōmona

eye in a closely tattooed place with a sharpened kō (digging implement), and the name is a pun: *moko* (tattoo); *kō* (digging implement). On the other hand, Mokoia, which was the original name for Panmure, was Mokoika, named after the taniwha (water-monster) Mokoikahikuwaru, the lizard with eight tails.

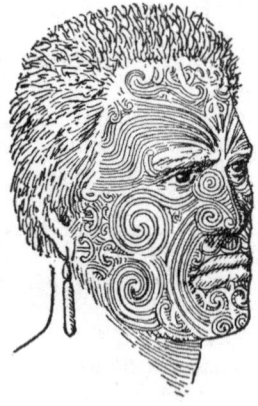

Moko: tattoo

Mōmona Good, fertile land.
Momorangi *momo* (offspring); *rangi* (the sky). Offspring of heaven.
Monowai The proper name is Manokiwai. *Mano* (a fixed channel); *kī* (full); *wai* (water). Channel full of water. It is a long narrow lake that is always full, although it receives no big streams or rivers. Monowai was as close as James McKerrow, the Pākehā discoverer, could get to the Māori name.
Mōrere A swing, or 'giant stride'.
Mororimu *moro* (wave); *rimu* (bull kelp). Kelp floating on the waves. A Māori chief who raided the pā reported his success by saying, 'Nothing now moves at Waipapa but the kelp in the sea.'
Motatau Talking to oneself. In this place Īhenga was heard talking to himself.
Mōtītī Literally, eliminated. Named after a place in Hawaiki because there was no firewood there. There is a proverb that concerns the Arawa canoe: Kei Mōtītī koe e noho ana: I suppose you are at Mōtītī, as you can find no firewood.
Motu Island, or isolated clump of trees.
Motuara *motu* (island); *ara* (path). Island in the path of the canoe.
Motuarohia *motu* (island); *arohia* (reconnoitred). The island that was spied upon.
Motueka In full, Motuweka. *Motu* (clump of trees); *weka* (wood-hen). Wood-hens in a grove of trees. The name originally came from Hawaiki, where it may have had a different connotation. It is sometimes said

to mean The crippled wood-hen — one of which was kept as a lure to capture weka.

Motuhorā Whale Island. This is the name given to it by Pākehā, in which case it should be Motutohorā. It could also mean *motu* (clumps of trees); *hora* (scattered). Scattered patches of bush.

Motuihe *motu* (island); *Ihe* (short for Īhenga). The island was named after Īhenga by his uncle Kahumatamomoe.

Motukanae *motu* (island); *kanae* (mullet). Mullet island.

Motukaraka *motu* (island); *karaka* (native tree). Island of the karaka trees.

Karaka: New Zealand tree

Motukārara *motu* (island); *kārara* (South Island form of *ngārara*: lizard). Lizard island.

Motukauatiiti *motu* (grove of trees); *kauati* (rubbing sticks to make fire); *iti* (little). Little fire-making tree grove. This was Corsair Bay, and Motukauatirahi (rahi meaning large) was Cass Bay. Both bays were noted for their groves of kaikōmako trees, the timber of which is specially suitable for fire-making.

Motukauatirahi See Motukauatiiti.

Motukauri *motu* (island); *kauri* (native tree). Kauri island. The small island in the Hokianga River was covered with kauri.

Motukiekie *motu* (island); *kiekie* (plant). This is the Māori name for Stop Island in Dusky Sound. It is one of the few places in the sound where the kiekie grows.

Motukina *motu* (island); *kina* (sea-egg). The island of sea-eggs.

Motukiore *motu* (island); *kiore* (rat). Rat island. The island at the mouth of the Motueka River was infested by rats, and had to be abandoned for cultivation.

Motunau *motu* (island); *nau* (scurvy grass). The grass grew here until it was eaten off by cattle.

Motunui *motu* (island); *nui* (big). Big island.

Motungārara *motu* (island); *ngārara* (lizard). Lizard island.

Motupiko *motu* (clump of

trees); *piko* (winding, or curved). Straggling clumps of trees.

Motupipi *motu* (island); *pipi* (shellfish). Pipi island.

Motupiu *motu* (island); *piu* (to swing). Swinging island. This is the Māori name for Dog Island, near Bluff. The story is that a southern tribe found a huge piece of greenstone in the sea. They drove it round to Bluff by following it in three canoes. It nearly eluded them several times and finally came to rest, where it remained as an island.

Motupōhue *motu* (island); *pōhue* (convolvulus). The Māori name for Bluff and specifically Bluff Hill.

Motupōua *motu* (island); *pōua* (old man). Old man island. An old chief was buried on the summit of the hill.

Moturātā *motu* (island); *rātā* (native tree). Rātā island. Whale Island at Taieri Mouth and other places of this name were often bright with the scarlet blossoms of the rātā.

Moturau *motu* (island); *rau* (many, or a hundred). A hundred islands. The correct name for Lake Manapōuri.

Moturoa *motu* (island); *roa* (long, or tall). Long island. There are many places with this name. Moturoa is the largest of the islands in the Bay of Islands, whereas Moturoa in Queen Charlotte Sound is small, and there probably means Tall island.

Moturua *motu* (island); *rua* (two, or a pit). Two islands, Island with a pit.

Motutāiko *motu* (island); *tāiko* (mutton bird). Mutton-bird island.

Motutapu *motu* (island); *tapu* (sacred, or forbidden). Sacred island.

Motutara *motu* (island); *tara* (gull). Gull island. Motutara Island in Lake Rotorua is frequented by the tarāpunga, the little lake gull.

Motutawa *motu* (island); *tawa* (native tree). Tawa island.

Motutawaki *motu* (island); *tawaki* (big, or crested penguin). Penguin island. Māori name for Passage Island.

Motutere *motu* (island); *tere* (floating). Floating island. Among the places it is found, it is the Māori name for Castle Rock at Coromandel, which looks like an island floating in the sky when it is surrounded by mist.

Motutīeke *motu* (island); *tīeke* (saddleback). Saddleback island.

Mourea Remnant. A name that comes from the Society Islands.

Moutapu *mou* (island); *tapu* (sacred). On this island in the Grey River the Māori placed the bones of their dead in the branches of kahikatea, thus making them tapu.

Moutere Island.

Moutoa In full Motutoa. *Motu* (island); *toa* (warrior). An island where warriors fought.

Moutohorā See Motuhora.

Muri-aroha-o-Kahu *muri* (breeze); *aroha* (affection); *o* (of); *Kahu* (Kahumatamomoe). Kahumatamomoe came to a dividing of the river Waihou and rested. As he felt the soft breeze, words of affection came to his lips.

Murihiku *muri* (end); *hiku* (tail). End of the tail. So named because it is the southern end of the South Island.

Muritai *muri* (breeze); *tai* (tide). Sea breeze.

Muriwai *muri* (end); *wai* (water). Backwater, or the junction of streams.

Muriwhenua *muri* (end); *whenua* (land). End of the land; Land's end. Māori name for North Cape.

Murupara *muru* (to wipe off); *para* (mud). To wipe off the mud.

N

Naenae Sandfly.

Namu Sandfly.

Naumai Come!

Nehutai Sea spray.

Nihomanga *niho* (thorn); *manga* (stream). Thorny stream. Possibly also Nihomangā: Barracouta tooth.

Nihoniho Young shoots or buds.

Nihotupu *niho* (tooth); *tupu* (broken). Decayed or broken teeth. Nihotupu in Auckland commemorates a person.

Nīkau Native palm.

Nokomai A corruption of Nukumai. Move this way towards the person speaking.

Nūhaka A place name brought from Hawaiki. There is no English equivalent.

Nukuhou *nuku* (to move); *hou* (feather). Moving feather.

Nukunuku To move away.

Nukuroa Far-stretching land. An old name for the North Island.

NG

Ngaere Swamp

Ngāhape *ngā* (the); *hape* (hunchback, or cripple). The cripples.

Ngahere The forest.

Ngāhinapōuri *ngā* (the); *hina* (grey hair); *pōuri* (sad) or *hinapōuri* (very dark, very sad). The sorrowing old woman; or possibly a corruption of Ngāhinepōuri.

Ngāhinepōuri *ngā* (the); *hine* (women); *pōuri* (sad). The sorrowing women.

Ngā hine: the women

Ngaio A native tree.

Ngaionui *ngaio* (native tree); *nui* (big). The big ngaio.

Ngā-karikari-a-Rākaihautū *ngā* (the); *karikari* (excavations); *a* (of); *Rākaihautū* (South Island giant). The diggings of Rākaihautū. The great series of cold lakes in the South Island, which were supposed to have been dug by the ancestor and explorer Rākaihautū.

Ngākawau The shags.

Ngā-kurī-a-Hinepoupou *ngā* (the); *kurī* (dogs); *a* (of); *Hinepoupou*. Hinepoupou was famous for swimming across Raukawa Moana (Cook Strait).

Ngākuta Edible seaweed that was found at these bays.

Ngā-makawe-o-Māhu *ngā* (the); *makawe* (hair); *o* (of); *Māhu* (a chief who engaged the rainbow god in conflict). The hairs of Māhu. They are represented by the flax that grows on the cliff.

Ngāmatapōuri *ngā* (the); *matapōuri* (black teal).

Ngāmoana *ngā* (the); *moana* (pit-covers).

Ngāmoko *ngā* (the); *moko* (lizards).

Ngāmotu *ngā* (the); *motu* (islands). The original Māori name for New Plymouth.

Ngāone *ngā* (the); *one* (sands).

Ngāpaenga *ngā* (the); *paenga* (boundaries).

Ngā-pākihi-whakatekateka-a-Waitaha See Kā-pākihi-whakatekateka-a-Waitaha.

Ngāpara The name should really be Ngātēpara. *Ngā* (the); *tēpara* (tables). It is a Pākehā invention, the equivalent of tablelands.

Ngāpōhatu *ngā* (the); *pōhatu* (rocks). The rocks.

Ngā-pōito-o-Te-Kupenga-a-Taramainuku The floats of the net of Taramainuku. These are the islands of the Hauraki Gulf. See Te Kupenga-a-Taramainuku.

Ngāpuhi *ngā* (the); *puhi* (plumes). The decorative plumes at the bow of a war canoe. Also the name of the Northland tribe.

Ngāpuke *ngā* (the); *puke* (hills).

Ngāpuna *ngā* (the); *puna* (springs).

Ngāroma *ngā* (the); *roma* (currents).

Ngāroto *ngā* (the); *roto* (lakes).

Ngāruawāhia *ngā* (the); *rua* (pits); *wāhia* (broken into). The plundered kūmara pits. The local tribe was entertaining a large party of visitors, and the store-pits of kūmara (sweet potatoes) had to be broken into to provide sufficient food.

Ngātaki *ngā* (the); *taki* (flocks of whiteheads: birds).

Ngatamiro *ngata* (dry); *miro* (tree). Dry miro tree.

Ngātapa *ngā* (the); *tapa* (edges).

Ngātīmoti Belonging to Timothy. A Māori carved his name on a tree. The words were *na Timoti*, which means, Belonging to Timothy, but they were changed to Ngātīmoti because it looked more like a Māori word.

Ngātira *ngā* (the); *tira* (parties of travellers).

Ngātūāhu *ngā* (the); *tūāhu* (sacred places).

Ngā-tutu-māhanga-a-Kaukohea The twin tutu heads of Kaukohea. When crossing the summit of a hill, a chief killed a hawk that was flying over with a sweep of his club. Not to be outdone, the other, Kaukohea, made a slash at two tutu bushes growing there, and gave the name.

Ngāuranga *ngā* (the); *uranga* (people who came by canoe).

Ngāuruhoe The name of a slave girl of Ngātoroirangi who was thrown into the crater of this volcano to appease the gods.

There are also two literal translations. One is based on the story that Ngātoroirangi threw his grandson Hoe into the crater, and the plumes of smoke represent his hair. *Ngā* (the); *uru* (hairs); *Hoe* (Ngātoro's grandson). The hairs of Hoe. The other gives the meaning as *ngā* (the); *uru* (the act of arranging hot stones in a hangi: earth oven); *hoe* (to toss out). When the mountain is erupting it tosses out hot stones.

Ngāurukehu *ngā* (the); *urukehu* (fair-haired people). The place of this name in Nelson was The red hairs, because a chief likened the prolific growth of the flax to his own red hair.

Ngāwaka *ngā* (the); *waka* (canoes).

Ngāwapurua *ngā* (the); *awa* (waters); *purua* (blocked up). The blocked-up waters. An alternative, Ngāwaipūrua, meaning The meeting of the waters, has been suggested.

Ngāwari Soft.

Ngāwaro *ngā* (the); *waro* (burning coals).

Ngāwhā Boiling springs.

Ngāwhakapakoko *ngā* (the); *whakapakoko* (carved posts or palisades).

Ngāwhatu *ngā* (the); *whatu* (eyes). The meaning of Ngā-whatu-kaiponu (The Brothers Islands) in Cook Strait was The guardian eyes. When Māori passed these rocks they veiled

Ngāwhā: hot springs

the eyes of those who were passing them for the first time, as otherwise the voyagers would meet with disaster. Another version is that Kupe placed the eyeballs of the octopus he killed on the islands, which thus became a tapu or sacred place.

Ngawī To squeal.

Ngongotahā *ngongo* (to drink); *tahā* (calabash). To drink from a calabash. Īhenga ascended this mountain and met a fairy woman who gave him a drink from her calabash. Then he was afraid and ran away, but gave the name to the river and mountain.

Ngunguru To sigh or to groan.

Ngutunui *ngutu* (lip); *nui* (big). Big lips.

Ngutuwera *ngutu* (lip); *wera* (burnt). Burnt lips.

Ōakura The place of the flashing of the redness. Turi of the Aotea canoe had a red cloak, which when spread out at this place was a symbol of his mana (prestige).

Ōamaru The place of the god Maru.

Ōamuru The place of the flesh left to dry. The flesh of conquered warriors was brought here to be preserved.

Ōaonui *ō* (the place of); *ao* (cloud); *nui* (big). The place of a large cloud.

Ōaro *ō* (the place of); *aro* (bog). A boggy place.

Ōeo *ō* (the place of); *eo* (louse). The place of lice.

Ōhaeawai The place of thermal water.

Ōhai *ō* (the place of); *hai* (stone used in a game).

Ōhakeā *oha* (to repeat incantations); *keā* (a lie, or false). Imperfect incantations.

Ōhakune *ō* (the place of); *hakune* (to be careful). A place to be careful in. Hakune may be a personal name.

Ōhāriu The correct name is Ōwhāriu, The place to turn aside. Kupe turned aside here to dry the sails of his canoe.

Ōhau The location near Levin was named The place of Hau, a noted traveller or name-giver. His full name was Haupipi-a-nania. Elsewhere the name means Windy place. Ōhau Stream in Rotorua was the place of Īhenga's dog, Hau, who was drowned in a whirlpool. Lake Ōhau commemorates Hau, a companion of Rākaihautū.

Ōhaupō The place of Haupō. Or, *ō* (the place of); *hau* (wind); *pō* (night). The place of night winds.

Ōhawe *ō* (the place of); *hawe* (bend in a river or road).

Ohia To approve, or to think on the spur of the moment.

Ohikanui To perform rites with incantations. Two bands of warriors separated here, and one party was provided with food. The incantations were chanted to secure their return.

Ōhinehoe The place of Hinehoe.

Ōhinekōpiri *ō* (the place of); *hine* (girl); *kōpiri* (shrivelled). The place of a young girl. Her name was

Punohu. She was assaulted, and her father died in her defence. Her body was hidden in a kūmara pit, but was revealed by the presence of hawks, and she was avenged.

Ōhinemutu *ō* (the place of); *hine* (girl); *mutu* (cut off). The place of the young woman who was killed. Hinetekakara (the fragrant maid) was the daughter of Īhenga. She was killed and her remains thrown into Lake Rotorua. To mark the place of her death, Īhenga set up a memorial stone and called it Ōhinemutu.

Ōhinepanea The place of Hinepanea.

Ōhinerau The place of Hinerau. She was a female goddess of whirlwinds.

Ōhinerēhia The place of Hinerēhia, a legendary mermaid.

Ōhinetahi The place of one daughter (daughter of Manuwhiri).

Ōhinewai The place of Hinewai. Literally, The place of the water girl.

Ōhingahape The place of the crooked foot. Named by Tiri after the crooked foot of Tuanui-a-te-rā.

Ōhingaiti The place of Hingaiti. Alternatively, *ohinga* (childhood); *iti* (small, or unimportant).

Ōhiro *ō* (the place of); *hiro* (dark, or stormy). A stormy place. The correct spelling is Ōwhiro, possibly after Whiro, the explorer.

Ōhiwa *ō* (the place of); *hiwa* (watchful, or alert). The place of watching.

Ōhoka *ō* (the place of); *hoka* (stake to which a decoy parrot is tied).

Ōhotu The place of Hotu. Literally, *ō* (the place of); *hotu* (the fifteenth night of the moon).

Ōhoukākā *ō* (the place of); *hou kākā* (parrot feather). The place of the parrot's feather. Īhenga took a feather from his hair and stuck it in the ground, and it became a taniwha (monster).

Ōhura The place of Hura. Literally, *ō* (the place of); *hura* (to uncover).

Ōihi *ō* (the place of); *ihi* (power, or authority).

Ōio *ō* (the place of); *io* (a spur).

Ōkā *ō* (the place of); *kā* (to burn). The place of burning or cooking. This was Shelly Beach, Auckland. Great catches of fish were made in the Waitematā and the people camped on the beach and kept the cooking fires going.

Ōkāhau *ō* (the place of); *Kāhau* (a famous greenstone weapon).

Ōkahu *ō* (the place of); *Kahu* (abbreviation of Kahumatamomoe).

Ōkahukura *ō* (the place of); *Kahukura*. The place of Kahukura, the god of the rainbow.

Ōkaiawa *ō* (the place of); *kai* (food); *awa* (river). The place of food by the river, or in the valley.

Ōkaihau *ō* (the place of); *kaihau* (vagabond). Literally, one who eats wind.

Ōkarahia The place of calling in vain. Some fugitives were surprised and killed here.

Ōkaramio Correctly, Ōkuramio, the place of the plume of the miromiro (tomtit).

Ōkareka *ō* (food for a journey); *kareka* (sweet). Tasty food for travellers.

Ōkārito *ō* (the place of); *kārito* (bulrush). A place where bulrushes grow plentifully.

Ōkataina *ō* (the place of); *kataina* (laughter). The place of laughing. The full name is Te Moana-i-kataina-e-Te-Rangitakaroro, The ocean laughed at by Te Rangitakaroro. He may well have laughed at the tiny lake Ōkataina being described as an ocean.

Ōkato The place of Kato. Literally, The place of the tidal wave, or the full-flowing tide.

Ōkau *ō* (the place of); *kau* (swimming or wading). The swimming place.

Ōkauia The place of Kauia. Literally, The place of articles threaded on a stick.

Ōkere *ō* (the place of); *kere* (to drift, or float).

Ōketeupoko *ō* (the place of); *kete* (basket); *upoko* (head). The place where baskets full of human heads were kept. The famous warrior Te Rangiwhakaputa captured the locality of Lyttelton from Ngāti Māmoe and kept the heads of the slain in baskets.

Ōkiato *ō* (the place of); *kiato* (a receptacle for holding sacred objects).

Ōkiore *ō* (the place of); *kiore* (rat).

Ōkiwi *ō* (the place of); *kiwi* (flightless bird). The place of the kiwi.

Kiwi: flightless bird

Ōkoke *ō* (the place of); *koke* (moving forwards).

Ōkoki *ō* (the place of); *koki* (small canoe).

Ōkonga *ō* (the place of); *konga* (running waters).

Ōkoroire *ō* (the place of); *koroire* (an extinct duck, which once was plentiful here).

Okowhiu *oko* (wooden bowl); *whiu* (to throw, or place). To place a wooden bowl. A name from the Ārai-te-uru canoe.

Ōkūī The place of Kūī. He was supposed to be one of the first people to live in Aotearoa, and was an immediate descendant of Tuputupuwhenua, who was left here by Māui. Literally *ō* (the place of); *kūī* (an underground insect).

Ōkuku *o* (the place of); *kuku* (shining cuckoo). The Pākehā called the place Cuckoo Hills and this was changed to the 'Māori' form, Ōkuku. Kuku is not the wood pigeon, therefore, but the shining cuckoo.

Ōkupe *ō* (the place of); *Kupe* (the famous explorer).

Ōkupu *ō* (the place of); *kupu* (message).

Ōkurī *ō* (the place of); *kurī* (dog).

Ōkuru *ō* (the place of); *kuru* (weary). The place of weariness.

Ōmāhanui *ō* (the place of); *māha* (pleasure); *nui* (great). The place of happiness.

Ōmahu The place of Mahu. Literally, The place of healing.

Ōmāhuri *ō* (the place of); *māhuri* (young trees).

Ōmahuta *ō* (the place of); *mahuta* (to rise). The place of rising, or landing from a canoe.

Ōmāio *ō* (the place of); *māio* (calm). A calm spot.

Ōmaka *ō* (the place of); *maka* (South Island form of *manga*: stream).

Ōmakau Belonging to husband and wife, i.e., the baby. There are three rocks in this Otago locality, the father, mother, and the smallest, Ōmakau.

Ōmāmari The place of the Māmari canoe. This famous canoe, which came from Hawaiki, was wrecked at Maunganui Bluff, and is petrified as a group of rocks.

Ōmanaia *ō* (the place of); *manaia* (carved figure with beak).

Ōmānawa *ō* (the place of); *mānawa* (mangrove).

Ōmanu *ō* (the place of); *manu* (birds).

Ōmāpere *ō* (the place of); *māpere* (a species of toetoe; plume grass).

Ōmarama The place of Marama. Literally, *ō* (the place of); *marama* (moon, or light).

Ōmatā *ō* (the place of); *matā* (quartz).

Ōmāui *ō* (the place of); *Māui* (the great explorer).

Ōmihi *ō* (the place of); *mihi* (lamentations). The place of this name in Canterbury was originally Ōmimi.

Ōmimi *ō* (the place of); *mimi* (a stream).

Ōmoana *ō* (the place of); *moana* (the ocean).

Ōmokoroa The place of Mokoroa. Literally, *ō* (the place of); *mokoroa* (a large white grub)

Ōnaeroa *ō* (the place of); *naeroa* (mosquito).

Ōnamalutu Obviously an incorrect spelling. It is possibly Ōnamahutu, the place of a cave, and it has been suggested that as the entrance to the valley is narrow, it has something of the appearance of a cave.

Ōnawe The place set on fire. It may refer to when Te Rauparaha set fire to this village on the Ōnawe Peninsula in Akaroa Harbour.

Ōnehunga *ō* (the place of); *nehunga* (burial). There were burial places on the shore.

Onekakā *one* (sand); *kakā* (hot). A descriptive name.

Onekakara *one* (beach); *kakara* (cockle shell, or smelly). Either Cockle shell beach, or Smelly beach. As the beach at Waikouaiti was part of a whaling station, it would have had an evil smell.

Onepoto *one* (beach); *poto* (short). Short, sandy beach.

Onepū *one* (sand); *pū* (loose). Loose sand.

Onepua Foam of the sea.

Onerahi *one* (beach); *rahi* (extensive). Long, sandy beach.

Oneroa *one* (beach); *roa* (long). Long beach.

Onetahua *one* (sand); *tahua* (heaped up). The name for Farewell Spit, and the sand dunes.

Onetahuti *one* (sand); *tahuti* (to run along). Running along the beach.

Onetangi *one* (sand); *tangi* (sounding). The sounding sands.

Onetapu *one* (sand); *tapu* (sacred). Sacred sand.

Onetea *one* (sand); *tea* (white). White sand.

Onewhero *one* (beach); *whero* (red). Red beach.

Ōniao *ō* (the place of); *niao* (gunwale of a canoe).

Ōnoke *ō* (the place of); *noke* (earthworm).

Ongaonga Nettle.

Ōngāroto *ō* (the place of); *ngā* (the); *roto* (lakes). The place of the lakes.

Ōngarue *ō* (the place of); *ngarue* (shaking, as in an earthquake).

Ōpaheke *ō* (the place of); *paheke* (slip). The place where the slip occurred.

Ōpaki *ō* (the place of); *paki* (fine weather).

Ōpapa *ō* (the place of); *papa* (flat land).

Ōpara *ō* (the place of); *para* (mud). Muddy place.

Ōpārae *ō* (the place of); *pārae* (open country).

Ōparapara *ō* (the place of); *parapara* (scum on the beach).

Ōpārara *ō* (the place of); *pārara* (to lie open towards). The shallow bay faces the Tasman Sea.

Ōpārau *ō* (the place of); *pā* (fortified village); *rau* (many). The place of many fortified villages.

Ōpatu *ō* (the place of); *patu* (to strike). The place of striking.

Ōpawa The correct form of the name is Ōpāwaho, the place of

Pā: fortified village

the outer or seaward pā (village). This is the meaning of the name of Ōpawa in Christchurch. The Ōpawa River in Marlborough is said to be Ōpaoa, Smoky river, because the brown swamp water that poured into it gave it this appearance.

Ōpepe *ō* (the place of); *pepe* (moth).

Ōpihi *ō* (the place of); *pihi* (springing up, referring to plants). The place of good growth.

Ōpoho The place of Poho. Literally, *ō* (the place of); *poho* (chest, or stomach).

Ōponae *ō* (the place of); *ponae* (a small basket).

Ōpononi The place of Pononi.

Ōpōtiki The place of Pōtiki. He

was Pōtiki-mai-tawhiti, Pōtiki from afar. Literally, The place of children.

Ōpōuri *ō* (the place of); *pōuri* (sadness).

Ōpoutama The place of Poutama. Literally, *ō* (the place of); *poutama* (pattern on the reed walls of a house).

Poutama: reed pattern

Ōpoutere *ō* (the place of); *pou* (post); *tere* (to float). The place of the floating post.

Ōpua The place of Pua. Literally, *ō* (the place of); *pua* (flower).

Ōpuatia *ō* (the place of); *pua* (flowers); *tia* (to stick in). The place of adorning with flowers.

Ōpunake The place of Punake. Literally *ō* (the place of); *punake* (bow of a canoe).

Ōpura *ō* (the place of); *pura* (dust in the eye). The place where Tamatea got dust in his eye.

Ōpūrere The place of flying mist.

Ōrākau *ō* (the place of); *rākau* (trees).

Ōrākei *ō* (the place of); *rākei* (adorning).

Ōrākeikōrako *ō* (the place of); *rākei* (adorning); *kōrako* (white sinter). This beautiful hot pool with its glowing colours was used as a place where chiefs attended to their toilet.

Orana Correctly Oranga: welfare.

Oranoa Escaping with difficulty.

Orapiu *ora* (alive, or escaped); *piu* (to throw).

Ōrarī The place of Rarī. Literally, *ō* (the place of); *rarī* (a fish).

Ōrātia *ō* (the place of); *rā* (sun); *tia* (persistency). The place of the long-lingering sun.

Orawaite See Orowaiti.

Orepuki Favourable weather; or a corruption of Aropaki (cliff) or Aropuke (swelling up), which can be rendered as Cliff washed by high tides.

Ōrere *ō* (the place of); *rere* (the waterfall, or low tide).

Ōreti *ō* (the place of); *reti* (a snare).

Ōrewa *ō* (the place of); *rewa* (the rewa shrub).

Orikākā *ori* (to wave to and fro); *kākā* (native parrot). To wave to attract the kākā. One method of snaring the kākā was to wave a piece of coloured fabric to attract the attention of the inquisitive bird, which was then easily caught. The Orikākā River was a place noted for birds.

Orikaroro *ori* (bad weather); *karoro* (sea-gull). Where sea-gulls congregate in bad weather.

Ōrini See Ōringi.

Ōringi The place of Ringi. The inhabitants of a besieged pā near Dannevirke included a beautiful young woman who was admired by Takarangi of another tribe. When he heard that the defenders were short of water he walked boldly to the palisades with a calabash of water for the young woman. This ultimately brought peace, and joy to the lovers. At the spring there was once a sign that read, 'Ko te Puna o Ringi' (Being the spring of Ringi).

Other places of this name probably mean *ō* (the place of); *ringi* (to pour out). The place of pouring out. Ōrini has the same meaning.

Ōrongo *ō* (the place of); *rongo* (round bay).

Ōrongorongo Correctly, Te Wai-o-Rongorongo. *Te* (the); *wai* (water, or stream); *o* (of); *Rongorongo* (the name of a woman). The stream of Rongorongo.

Ōropi *ō* (the place of); *ropi* (to cover up). The place of concealment. It may also be a Māori form of Europe.

Ōroroa *ō* (the place of); *roroa* (a shellfish).

Ōrotore *ō* (the place of); *roto* (inside); *re* (short for *repo*: swamp). The swamp dwellers. This was an almost humorous term applied to the Māori who lived along the banks of the River Avon in Christchurch. Although they lived in a swampy region they were well provided with eels and ducks.

Ōrotorepo See Ōrotore.

Orowaiti When Reuben Waite, the first store-keeper on the West Coast, arrived with supplies for the gold-diggers, the Māori called joyfully, 'Ora, Waite!' This may be a contraction of 'Kia ora, Waite!' Welcome Waite.

Another explanation is that the name may originally have been Oraiti: escaping with difficulty.

Ōrua *ō* (the place of); *rua* (a pit).

Ōruaiti *ō* (the place of); *rua* (pit); *iti* (little). The place of the little pit.

Ōruaiwi *ō* (the place of); *rua* (two, or pit); *iwi* (bone). The place of the pit containing bones.

Ōruanui *ō* (the place of); *rua* (pit); *nui* (big). The place of the large pit.

Ōruawairua *ō* (the place of); *rua* (two); *wairua* (soul, or spirit). Rua wairua may have been a name for an urupā (burial ground).

Ōruru *ō* (the place of); *ruru* (morepork).

Ōrurutūmārō The immovable owl, the legendary name of a guardian of cultivations.

Otago Correctly, **Ōtākou**; *ō* (the place of); *tākou* (red earth, or red ochre). The Otago Peninsula abounded in yellow earth that yielded red ochre when burnt. The southern pronunciation of 'k' approaches 'g' in sound. The name was extended from the Kaik near Taiaroa Head to the harbour, and finally to the province.

Ōtahāiiti The place of the little calabash.

Ōtahu *ō* (the place of); *tahu* (signal fire). The local people used to light fires on the peak to warn their neighbours of the approach of raiding parties.

Otahuhu *ota* (uncooked); *huhu* (grub). Eating of the huhu grub in an uncooked state. This was done by Waikato Māori who, on dragging their canoes across the portage, discovered several rotten tree trunks full of huhu grubs. Alternatively, **Ōtāhuhu**, Place of the ridgepole.

Otahuti *ota* (uncooked); *huti* (to pull out of the ground).

Ōtāika *ō* (the place of); *tāika* (to lie in a heap); or **Otaika**: *ota* (to eat raw); *ika* (fish).

Ōtākaro *ō* (the place of); *tākaro* (games or sports). The place of the sport. The original name of the Avon River, and the site of Hagley Park.

Ōtaki *ō* (the place of); *taki* (to stick in). The place where the staff

Ruru: morepork

was stuck in the ground by Hau, who was pursuing his wife.

Ōtākiri *ō* (the place of); *tākiri* (loosening, or making free of tapu).

Ōtaku *ō* (the place of); *taku* (slow and deliberate, or firm and solid).

Ōtakuwao The place where a bird was seen flying past a belt of trees.

Ōtamahua *ō* (the place of); *tama* (short for *tamariki*: children); *hua* (eggs). The place where children ate sea-gulls' eggs. This was the Māori name for Quail Island, where the gulls' eggs were a delicacy much esteemed by children as well as adults.

Otamangō *ota* (uncooked); *mangō* (shark).

Ōtamarākau *ō* (the place of); *tama rākau* (warriors, or the young men who carry weapons).

Ōtamarau *ō* (the place of); *Tamarau* (a legendary spirit who comes in whirlwinds).

Otamātāpio *ota* (uncooked); *mātā* (a plant); *pio* (many).

Ōtanamomo Correctly, Ōtānemoamoa. *ō* (the place of); *tāne* (man); *moamoa* (spherical stone).

Ōtāne The moon on the 27th day, or, The place of man.

Ōtānenui *ō* (the place of); *tāne* (man); *nui* (big). The place of the big man.

Ōtāneuru *ō* (the place of); *tāne* (man); *uru* (to gather berries). The place where the man gathered berries.

Ōtangaroa *ō* (the place of); *Tangaroa* (god of the sea).

Ōtangihaku *ō* (the place of); *tangi* (to cry or lament); *haku* (to murmur).

Ōtangiwai *ō* (the place of); *tangi* (to sound, or weep); *wai* (water). The place of sounding or weeping waters.

Ōtara *ō* (the place of); *tara* (mountain peak, or spear).

Ōtaraia The place of Taraia, a Waitaha chief.

Ōtari *ō* (the place of); *tari* (snare). The place of bird snares. Wilton and Tinakori Hill were places noted for birds.

Ōtatara *ō* (the place of); *tatara* (to untie or loosen). Or **Otatara**: *ota* (unripe); *tara* (point). Green point has been suggested as the meaning, but this is unlikely.

Ōtaua *ō* (the place of); *taua* (war party).

Ōtautahi *ō* (the place of); *Tautahi* (short for a personal name, Te Pōtikitautahi). The Māori name for Christchurch commemorates the chief who had his pa beside a ford on the Avon River. The name refers also to the Avon River.

Ōtautau The place of Tautau. Literally, *ō* (the place of); *tautau* (greenstone ear-pendant with curved lower end).

Otautu *ota* (raw); *utu* (revenge). Raw revenge. After a battle fought to avenge a wrong, the victors ate the bodies of the vanquished raw.

Ōtawa *ō* (the place of); *tawa* (native tree). The place of tawa trees.

Ōtekaieke *ō* (of); *te* (the); *kaieke* (going around).

Ōtekura *ō* (the place of); *te* (the); *kura* (red feather). The place of the red feather.

Ōtematatā The place of good quartz or flint.

Ōtepopo The place of Te Popo. Literally, the place of the decay.

Ōtepoti *ō* (the place of); *te* (the); *poti* (corner, angle). The place situated at a corner. The Māori name for Dunedin is taken from a village that was located just south of the modern Octagon.

Ōtetī *ō* (the place of); *te* (the); *tī* (cabbage-tree). The place of the cabbage-tree.

Ōteuku *ō* (the place of); *te* (the); *uku* (white clay).

Ōtewā *ō* (the place of); *te* (the); *wā* (open country).

Ōtiake Correctly, Ōtiaki. *ō* (the place of); *tiaki* (to watch for). The place of watching.

Ōtiki The place of the tiki (image) of Marokura.

Ōtipua *ō* (the place of); *tipua* (goblin).

Ōtira *ō* (the place of); *tira* (a company of travellers). There was an old camping place on the Ōtira River where food was prepared for the journey over the ranges by the Hurunui Pass.

Ōtiria *ō* (the place of); *tiria* (to be planted).

Ōtītaha *ō* (the place of); *tītaha* (the axe).

Ōtōkia The place of Tōkia. Literally, *ō* (the place of); *tōkia* (to be wet).

Ōtoko *ō* (the place of); *toko* (a stick).

Ōtonga *ō* (the place of); *tonga* (the south).

Ōtoroa The place of Toroa (a chief).

Ōtorohanga *ō* (food for a journey); *torohanga* (to cause to extend over a distance). Food eked out. A chief who was going

Toroa: albatross

to Taupō carried only a small quantity of food, which he made last out the journey by means of magic spells.

Ōtōtara *ō* (the place of); *tōtara* (tree).

Ōtuhi *ō* (the place of); *tuhi* (smell of decaying fish).

Ōtūkoroiti Correctly, Ōkoroiti, the moon on the fifth day of the month. A fight that took place here began at sunrise on the fifth day and ended only when the moon rose.

Ōtūmahana The place of warm, still waters.

Ōtūmoetai The tide standing still as if asleep.

Otupaka *otu* (dried or scorched); *paka* (girdle).

Ōtūrehua *ō* (the place of); *tū* (to stand); *rehua* (a star). The place where the summer star stands high in the heavens, i.e., a place where it is very warm.

Ōtūtahanga *ō* (the place of); *tū* (to stand); *tahanga* (naked). The place of standing naked.

Ōue The place of Ue or Ui, who came to the South Island with Māui. Literally, a species of flax, or the moon on the fourth night.

Ōuruhia *ō* (the place of); *uruhia* (to be attacked).

Ōwahanga *ō* (the place of); *wahanga* (the entrance). The mouth of the river.

Ōwairaka The place of Wairaka, or the water of Raka.

Ōwairoa *ō* (the place of); *wai* (water); *roa* (long). The place of the long river, an old name for Howick.

Ōwaka *ō* (the place of); *waka* (canoe, or trough).

Ōwānanga The place of the historical recitals.

Ōwē *ō* (the place of); *Wī* or *Wē* (proper name), who came to the South Island with Māui.

Ōweka *ō* (the place of); *weka* (wood-hen). The place where the weka is plentiful.

Ōwhakatihi *ō* (the place of); *whakatihi* (to pile up in a heap).

Ōwhango

The sons of Tūwharetoa ranged over the Kaingaroa Plain in search of someone to attack, but when they met a party of Māori they were defeated, and their bodies were piled up in a heap at the foot of a tree.

Ōwhango *ō* (the place of); *whango* (hoarse or nasal sound).

Ōwhāroa *ō* (food for a journey); *whāroa* (lasting a long time). It has much the same meaning as Ōtorohanga.

Ōwhata *ō* (the place of); *whata* (a food store).

Ōwhiro *ō* (the place of); *whiro* (a moonless night, or the god of darkness).

Ōwhitiangaterā *ō* (the place of); *whitianga* (shining); *te* (the); *rā* (sun). The place of the shining sun.

Waka: canoe

P

Pā Fortified village. The name usually occurs in places named by Pākehā, such as Pā Flat. Pā can also mean a clump (of plants) or a flock (of birds).

Paehinahina *pae* (headland); *hinahina* (whitey-wood). Headland clothed with hinahina, māhoe, or whitey-wood trees.

Paekākāriki *pae* (perch); *kākāriki* (parakeet). The perch of parakeets. There is a legend that Hau, who was pursuing his wife, came to a barrier of rock at the south end of the beach, which gave the name to the place. He made a hole in the cliff with his taiaha, and walked through to the other side, where he found his wife.

Paekohu The place of fogs.

Paenga Boundary, or the margin of the kūmara plantations.

Paengaroa *paenga* (boundary); *roa* (long). Long boundary or margin.

Paerātā *pae* (ridge); *rātā* (tree). The ridge of the rātā tree. A large rātā stood here for many years, most of the surrounding trees being pūriri.

Paerau *pae* (step, or ridge); *rau* (a hundred, or many). A hundred ridges.

Paeroa *pae* (ridge, or range); *roa* (long). Long mountain range.

Paetawa *pae* (bird-snare); *tawa* (native tree). The tawa tree containing a bird-snare.

Paewhenua *paewhenua* (dock, or long-rooted weed); *whenua* (country). Noxious weed country. Paewhenua can also mean Expanse of land.

Pāharakeke *pā* (clump); *harakeke* (flax). Clump of flax.

Pāhau Beard, or the withered, drooping lower leaves of the cabbage-tree.

Pāhautāne Correctly, Pāhautaniwha. *Pāhau* (whale-bone); *taniwha* (large fish). A war party was retiring up the coast after a raid, and found that their concealed food-stores had been plundered. They camped for the night and the next morning found a school of blackfish stranded on the beach. In their hunger, they ate the flesh raw. Taniwha can refer to fish such as large sharks and whales, as well as monsters.

Pāhautea *pāhau* (beard); *tea* (white). White beard. The name of a tree, *Libocedrus bidwilli*.

Pahī Company of travellers.

Pāhia Slapped, or a preparation of mashed food.

Pahīatua *pahī* (resting place); *atua* (a god). The resting place of a god. A chief escaped from a fight, and was led by his atua on the flight till they came here and rested on the hill.

Pahītua *pahī* (company of travellers); *tua* (cut down). Party of travellers cut down.

Pāhoro The fall or capture of a pā.

Paiatepukahu *pai* (good); *a* (of); *te* (the); *pukahu* (abundant). The place of good, abundant food.

Paihia Good here. It is believed to be a word of mixed origin. The Reverend Henry Williams came to New Zealand knowing only a few words of Māori, including pai, which means good. When they came to this place he turned to his companion, a Māori chief, and said, 'Pai here.' It is possible that the name should be Pāhia.

Paire A bundle.

Pākarae *pā* (flock); *karae* (sea bird). Sea-bird village.

Pākaraka *pā* (clump); *karaka*

Pākawau · Papaaroha

(native tree). Clump of karaka trees.

Pākawau *pā* (flock, or colony); *kawau* (shag). Colony of shags.

Pākeha *pā* (garden plot); *keha* (indigenous white turnip). Plot where the turnip grows. One explanation of the name Pākehā is that it is one whose skin is white like that of a turnip. Other explanations are not so polite.

Pākihi Flat land, usually dried up and poor.

Pākihiroa *pākihi* (flat country); *roa* (long or broad). Large extent of pākihi.

Pākihikura *pākihi* (flat land); *kura* (red). Reddish coloured flat land.

Pakipaki An abbreviation of Pakipaki-o-Hinetemoa. This high-born young woman came to a stream accompanied by her slave girl. After she had bathed, her maid slapped (pakipaki) and massaged her body.

Pākira Bald head. Pākira-a-Hikawera was a place where a chief of this name was wearing a closely fitting hat of birds' feathers. Feeling hot, he took it off, and another chief exclaimed, 'What a beautiful bald head you have!'

Pakiri To grin.

Pakōtai *pakō* (to make a sudden sound); *tai* (the sea). Sudden sound from the sea.

Pākōwhai *pā* (clump); *kōwhai* (native tree). A clump of kōwhai, or the pā by the kōwhai trees. Or **Pakowhai** *pako* (to glean); *whai* (to search for). To look for remnants of the crop after it has been harvested.

Paku A small quantity.

Pakuranga *paku* (small quantity); *ranga* (company of persons, or shoal of fish). A small company, or a small shoal of fish.

Pamapuria The Māori pronunciation of Pamphylia, a locality named by the Reverend Joseph Matthews of Kaitāia.

Pānia The Pānia Reef at Napier is named after a woman of the sea people who married a chief.

Pāngaio *pā* (fortified village); *ngaio* (native tree). Pā near the ngaio trees.

Pangatōtara *panga* (thrown); *tōtara* (native tree). Probably named because a tōtara log was left here after a flood.

Panguru To make a rumbling sound.

Papaaroha *papa* (foundation); *aroha* (love, or affection). The foundation of love. A meeting place for many scattered sub-tribes.

Pāpāhaoa A variety of kūmara.

Papahīnau *papa* (undulating or nearly flat land); *hīnau* (a native shrub). Flat where the hīnau grows. Also known as Papahina, and Papahinu.

Papaioea Popularly believed to mean, How beautiful it is! Another explanation is, *papai* (exceedingly good); *oea* (the beauty that comes on the water when dead bodies are soaked in it). The Rangitāne people were said to soak the bodies of the slain in water before storing or eating them. Te Papaioea is the Māori name of Palmerston North.

Papaiti *papa* (flat); *iti* (little). Little flat.

Papakaio *papa* (flat); *kaio* (South Island form of *ngaio*). Ngaio flat.

Papaki A cliff against which the waves beat.

Papakura *papa* (flat); *kura* (red). Level land of red soil.

Papamoa *papa* (flat); *moa* (raised beds). Level land with raised plots for cultivation.

Papanui Big flat plain, or a stage in a tree used as a seat by a bird-snarer.

Paparātā *papa* (flat); *rātā* (native tree). Rātā flat.

Paparekareka *papa* (flat rock); *rekareka* (pleasant). The name would mean Pleasant flat, but Paparekareka is a bluff in North Otago.

Paparimu *papa* (flat); *rimu* (native tree). Rimu flat.

Paparoa Long flat rock, or large expanse of level land. Where the name refers to a headland it means long, flat, rocky point.

Papatawa *papa* (flat); *tawa* (native tree). Tawa flat.

Papatea Possibly named after the light-coloured papa-rock banks of the stream, or a term for a chief who was not tattooed.

Papatoetoe *papa* (flat); *toetoe* (pampas grass). Toetoe flat.

Papatōtara *papa* (flat); *tōtara* (native tree). Tōtara flat.

Papatōwai *papa* (flat); *tōwai* (native tree). Tōwai (or kāmahi) flat.

Papawai *papa* (flat land); *wai* (water). Inundated land.

Papaweka *papa* (flat); *weka* (wood-hen). Weka run, or fowl run. It sometimes appears as Tāpapaweka.

Pāponga *pā* (fortified village); *ponga* (fern). Pā by the fern trees.

Para A type of fern, or possibly swamp.

Pāraharaha The name comes from a pool of black mud in which flax fibre was dyed.

Parahaki A corruption of Parahaka. The Parawhau tribe had a large pā on the summit. They were invaded and defeated, and the conquerors danced a haka either in triumph or prior to inviting the Parawhau to surrender. Parahaka is a contraction of Parawhau and haka.

Parahau Windy place.

Parakai *para* (fern-root); *kai* (food, or to eat).

Parakakau *para* (fern); *kakau* (stalk). Fern-stalk.

Parakao Dried kūmara.

Paranui *para* (fern); *nui* (big, or plenty). Plenty of fern.

Parapara A name. Literally, soft mud used in dying flax fibre.

Paraparaumu *parapara* (scraps, or waste fragments); *umu* (earth oven in which scraps of food were found). A hungry taua (war party) captured a village but found only fragments of food in the oven. An earlier name may have been Paraparamāu, meaning First fruits for you.

Pararoa Possibly should be Parāoa, as it is said that it means whale, because one was washed ashore here long ago.

Paratetaitonga Dregs from the southern seas.

Pārau Slave.

Parawa *pā* (fortified village); *rawa* (property, or ground). Land on which the village was built.

Parawai A cloak, or sandal. The name comes from Tahiti and was given by Tamatekapua to his kūmara plantation in memory of those in the Pacific homeland.

Parekākāriki *pare* (plume); *kākāriki* (parakeet). Plume of the kākāriki.

Parekura Red ornamental band for the forehead.

Paremata A feast in return for one previously given.

Pāremoremo Hesitating, or slippery.

Parenga A riverbank, or possibly Parengo, slippery.

Pārengarenga The renga lily, or the place where the lily grows.

Pareora Life-giving, or bountiful. The name may originally have been Pureora, a sacred rite performed for the recovery of the sick.

Pārera Native duck.

Paretai Bank of a river.
Pariawhakatahakura *pari* (cliff); *a* (of); *whakataha* (to cause to change direction); *kura* (red). The red lichen-covered cliff that causes the river to change direction.
Parihaka Low cliff.
Parikārakaraka Echoing cliff.
Parikawa Abbreviated form of Parikawakawa. *Pari* (cliff); *kawakawa* (native tree). Cliff where the kawakawa grows.
Parikawau *pari* (cliff); *kawau* (shag). Shag cliff.
Pāringa *pā* (blow); *ringa* (hand). To strike a blow with the hand.
Parininihi *pari* (cliff); *ninihi* (lofty). Lofty cliff. The White Cliffs are 250 metres high.
Parinuioterā *pari* (cliff); *nui* (big); *o* (of); *te* (the); *rā* (sun). The big cliff shining in the sun.
Paripari Precipitous country.
Pariroa *pari* (cliff); *roa* (long, or tall). High cliff.
Pariruru *pari* (cliff); *ruru* (sheltered). Cliff that provides a shelter from the wind.
Paritea *pari* (cliff); *tea* (white). White or light-coloured cliff.
Paritutū *pari* (cliff); *tutū* (erect). Upright cliff.
Pariwhero *pari* (cliff); *whero* (red). Red cliff.
Pāroa *pā* (fortified village); *roa* (long). Spread out or straggling settlement.
Pārore Gentle, or friendly. The Northland locality is named after Pārore Te Āwhā, who died in 1887 when he was nearly 100; true to his name he was always friendly to Pākehā.
Pārua *pā* (fortified village); *rua* (pit, edge or two). Two pā, or the pit in the pā.
Paruāuku Soil of white clay.
Paruparu Black mud used in dying flax fibre.
Pātara Māori pronunciation of Butler (or bottle).
Pātea In full, Pātea-nui-a-Turi. The place where Turi's people threw down their great burdens.

Pataka: raised storehouse

Pātearoa Long fortification with a clear view (Pā wātea roa).

Pāterangi *pā* (fortified village); *te* (the); *rangi* (sky). The fort in the sky.

Pātetonga *pā* (fortified village); *te* (the); *tonga* (south wind). Village swept by the south wind.

Pātoka The pā in the rocks. The hill above the pā has great limestone formations.

Patumāhoe *patu* (weapon, or to strike); *māhoe* (timber of a native tree). In a battle at this place a chief was killed with a māhoe stake.

Pātūnga *pā* (fortified village); *tūnga* (being wounded). The place where someone was wounded.

Paturuahine *patu* (to strike); *ruahine* (old woman). The place where the old woman was struck.

Pātūtahi *pā* (fortified village); *tūtahi* (lonely). Lonely or isolated village.

Pāua Shellfish (*Haliotis sp.*).

Pāuanui Many pāua (shellfish).

Pāuatahanui *pāuātaha* (variety of kumara); *nui* (many).

Pehu Variety of kūmara, to pound, or to bend.

Peka Named after Peka Mākarini (Baker McLean).

Pekapekarau *pekapeka* (native bat); *rau* (many). The place where native bats were plentiful.

Pekatahi *peka* (branch); *tahi* (single). The single branch.

Pekerangi The outer palisades of a pā.

Pēowhairangi The Māori transliteration of Bay of Islands.

Pepeke Native butterfly.

Peraki Probably Pireka (the spelling adopted by the French), a type of fern, the root of which had a pleasant smell when pounded.

Peria Māori form of the Biblical Berea.

Pētane Māori pronunciation of Bethany. The name is now changed to Bay View to avoid confusion with Petone.

Peterehema Māori form of Bethlehem.

Petone A corruption of Pito-one. *Pito* (end); *one* (sandy beach). End of the beach.

Piaka Root of a tree, or weapon made from a root.

Piako Shrunk, or hollow. The name was brought from Hawaiki by the Tainui people.

Piha Ripple at the bow of a canoe.

Pīhama After Hone Pīhama (John Beecham).

Pīhautea See Pāhautea.

Pihanga Window. The mountain had an opening in its side like the smoke vent in a house.

Pīkaroro *pī* (nestling); *karoro* (sea-gull). Nestling of sea-gulls.

Pikopiko Winding.

Pikowai *piko* (curving); *wai* (water). Curving stream.

Pininoa A refuge, or hiding place.

Piopio Native thrush.

Piopiotahi *piopio* (thrush); *tahi* (single). A single thrush. The Māori name for Milford Sound. After Māui was defeated by the goddess of death, the thrush fled here sorrowing for its dead companion. Another legend says it is the name of a very early canoe.

Pipi Shellfish.

Pipikarita Shellfish for evil spirits.

Pipiriki *pipi* (shellfish); *riki* (little). Little pipi. An old chief who was dying asked for little pipi, and a canoe was sent to get them, but by the time they arrived back he was dead.

Pipiroa *pipi* (shellfish); *roa* (long, or many). Plenty of pipi.

Pipitea *pipi* (shellfish); *tea* (white). White shellfish.

Pīpīwai Damp, or swampy.

Pīpīwharauroa Shining cuckoo.

Piriaka *piri* (to cling); *aka* (vine). The clinging forest vines.

Pirinoa A parasitic plant.

Piripai The Māori form of Philippi.

Piripāua *piri* (clinging); *pāua* (shellfish). The clinging shellfish. They are plentiful in the two places in Marlborough with this name.

Piripiri A bur, commonly known as biddybid.

Pirongia The full name is Pirongia-te-aroaro-o-Kahu, meaning the health-restoring purification of Kahurere, whose husband restored her to health.

Pōhaturoa *pōhatu* (stone); *roa* (long). Long stones are found in the river bed in Westland. Elsewhere it means The tall rock.

Pōhāngina The warming of the ovens at night.

Pohokura The name of a chief. Literally, *poho* (breast); *kura* (red).

Pohonui The big haul.

Pohowahine *poho* (breast); *wahine* (woman). A woman's breast.

Pohowaikawa *poho* (breast); *waikawa* (bitter water).

Pōhuehue Climbing plant, such as convolvulus.

Pōhuenui *pōhue* (convolvulus);

nui (big, or many). Plenty of convolvulus.

Pōhutu Splashing. The famous geyser at Whakarewarewa.

Pōhutukawa Native tree with scarlet blossoms. The name is usually given by Pākehā, as in Pōhutukawa Flat.

Poka The name of a pet lizard lost at this place by Tamatea.

Pōkaikōkō Flock of tūī.

Pōkaiwhenua A wanderer across the land. It is a tributary of the Waikato River.

Pōkākā A tree related to the hīnau.

Pokapū Middle, or a house with the door in the middle of its side wall.

Pōkeno Turbid; or *pō* (night); *keno* (underworld). Night in the underworld.

Pokere Pulp of the tawa berry, or pitfall, or in the dark.

Pokohiwi Name of a chief. Literally, shoulder.

Pokopokoiere Native frog.

Pokororo Abbreviation for upokororo, native fish (grayling).

Pōmahaka Correctly, Poumahaka (posts to which snares are attached).

Pōmare Named after Sir Māui Pōmare.

Pōneke: Port Nicholson

Pōneke Māori form of Port Nick, a contraction of Port Nicholson. Pōneke is used commonly to refer to Wellington.

Pōnui *pō* (night); *nui* (big). Big night.

Ponga Tree-fern.

Pongakawa To devour. Also *ponga* (tree-fern); *kawa* (bitter).

Pongaroa Name of a game; or, *ponga* (tree-fern); *roa* (long, or, many). Plenty of tree-ferns.

Popoia A gathering together.

Pōpōtūnoa Correctly, Poupoutūnoa, a post set up to mark the boundaries between Ngāti Māmoe and Ngāi Tahu.

Poranui *pora* (flat-roofed); *nui* (big).

Pōrangahau *pō* (night); *rangahau* (pursuit). The inhabitants of Heretaunga once had to make a hasty retreat from their enemies to this place.

Porangarua The correct form of

Pōrangirangi

the name is Pungarehu, ashes left by the fire. Some fugitives were discovered here when the wind stirred up the ashes of their fire.

Pōrangirangi To annoy at night.

Porararī Correctly, Pororarī. *Poro* (broken off); *rarī* (uproar). The end of the uproar. The waters of the river would rise swiftly and turbulently, and recede as quickly.

Pōrewa Elevated platform or watch-tower.

Porirua The proper form is probably Parirua. *Pari* (flowing tide); *rua* (two). There are two arms in the harbour. It may also be named after the taniwha that was supposed to inhabit it.

Poro-o-Tarao The posterior of Tarao. The chief was climbing the range ahead of his companions with his rāpaki (waist-mat) kilted up, and the sight amused his companions who were below him.

Poroporo A plant with a blue flower.

Porotī A forest bird; or *poro* (to cut short); *tī* (cabbage-tree).

Pōtaka After the chief Utiku Pōtaka. Literally, a spinning top.

Pōteriteri Dripping wet. Or Poutiritiri, a post on which offerings are hung, which is the more likely meaning.

Poutū

Pōterīwhi Port of relief. Also a transliteration for Port Levy.

Pōtete A small bark basket.

Pouākai A fabulous gigantic bird.

Poukawa *pou* (post); *kawa* (lean). Lean pole. Of the two chiefs who lived by the lake, one was more powerful than the other. The lesser chief asked that their fishing boundaries be divided, but the great chief was insulted. Then the lesser chief put a pole dividing the boundary, giving himself the best part of the lake, and leaving the tuna kawa (lean eels) for the other. The lake was then called Lean pole. Much strife followed.

Poukino *pou* (post); *kino* (bad).

Pounamu Greenstone.

Pounawea *pou* (post); *nawea* (to set on fire). Post that was set on fire.

Poutini A form of greenstone. It is the 'fish' Kupe (or Ngahue/Kahue) brought with him from Hawaiki. The name can refer to the whole of the West Coast.

Pōuto To cut off.

Poutū *pou* (staff); *tū* (to stand). Staff standing up. When Tamatea reached this place on the east side of Lake Taupō, he rested on his staff while he surveyed the district.

Pōwaru *pō* (night); *waru* (eight). Eight nights. Tamatea and his men dragged their canoe overland from the headwaters of the Whanganui to Lake Taupō. At this place they were unable to obtain provisions and had to go for eight days and nights without food.

Pūaha Mouth of a river.

Puatai Foam of the sea.

Puha A war song, or **Pūhā**, a wild vegetable.

Puhinui *puhi* (plumes); *nui* (big). Great plume at the bow of a canoe. It is the name of a canoe, and the settlement near Papatoetoe. It is also an early name for Warkworth, where it means Great promise, i.e., engagement or betrothal.

Pūhoi Slow water, so called because the tide is very slow in creeping up the river to make it navigable for canoes.

Pūkaha Spongy or swampy.

Pūkaki Head of the creek, or where the stream meets the tidal waters. Lake Pūkaki may have this meaning, but there is a legend that Rākaihautū (who scooped out the southern lakes) saw its bulging outlet and called it *pū* (heaped or bunched up), and *kakī* (neck).

Pukapuka Shrub with white leaves.

Pūkaramū A clump of karamū trees.

Pukatea A native tree.

Pukearuhe *puke* (hill); *aruhe* (fern-root). Hill where fern-root may be found.

Pukeatua *puke* (hill); *atua* (god). The hill of the god.

Pukehāpopo *puke* (hill); *hāpopo* (corpse of an enemy). The hill of the enemy corpse. A name that comes from the Society Islands.

Pukehiki *puke* (hill); *hiki* (charm to raise anything from the water). Hill of the incantation.

Pukehina *puke* (hill); *hina*, or *hinahina* (small tree, māhoe, or whitey-wood). Hill of the māhoe tree.

Pukehīnau *puke* (hill); *hīnau* (native tree). Hill of the hīnau trees.

Pukehiwitahi *puke* (hill); *hiwi* (peak); *tahi* (single). Hill with a single peak. It was named after the captain of the Ārai-te-uru canoe. The name was rendered as Pukeviti by early Pākehā settlers.

Pukehou *puke* (hill); *hou* (short for *houhou*: small flowering tree). Hill of the houhou trees. Pukehou in Horowhenua is the hill of dedication, where a boy was dedicated to the recovery of his tribal lands.

Pukehuhu *puke* (hill); *huhu* (grub). Hill where the huhu grubs were to be found.

Pukehuia *puke* (hill); *huia* (extinct bird). Hill of the huia.

Pukekākāriki *puke* (hill); *kākāriki* (parakeet). Hill of the parakeets.

Pukekāhu *puke* (hill); *kāhu* (hawk). Hill of the hawks.

Pukekaihau *puke* (hill); *kaihau* (a ceremony performed over successful warriors when they return). Hill where victory is celebrated.

Pukekāpia *puke* (hill); *kāpia* (kauri gum). Kauri gum hill.

Pukekaroro *puke* (hill); *karoro* (sea-gull). Hill where the sea-gulls gather. It was a fortified hill that frequently changed hands, and after each battle the sea-gulls gathered in their thousands.

Pūkeko A swamp bird.

Pukekohe *puke* (hill); *kohe* (*kohekohe*: a native tree). Hill where the kohekohe tree grows.

Pukekoikoi *puke* (hill); *koikoi* (pointed). Pointed hills, or a sharp-ridged hill.

Pukekōmā *puke* (hill); *kōmā* (light-coloured). A hill that is light in colour.

Pukekura *puke* (hill); *kura* (red). Red hill.

Pukekurī *puke* (hill); *kurī* (dog). Hill of dogs.

Pukemāeroero *puke* (hill); *māeroero* (wild men). Hill of the wild men.

Pukemaire *puke* (hill); *maire* (native tree). Maire hill.

Pukemakariri *puke* (hill); *makariri* (cold). Cold hill.

Pukemāori *puke* (hill); *Māori* (native). Māori hill.

Pukemata *puke* (hill); *mata* (headland). The hill on the headland.

Pukemātāwai *puke* (hill); *mātāwai* (source of waters). The hill that is the source of several streams or rivers. This name was given in modern times because the hill in the Tararua Range is the source of a number of rivers.

Pukemiro *puke* (hill); *miro* (native tree). Miro hill.

Pukemoa *puke* (hill); *moa* (giant extinct bird). Moa hill. So named because it was a haunt of the moa long ago, as is shown by the presence of bones.

Pukenamu *puke* (hill); *namu* (sandfly). Sandfly hill.

Pukenui *puke* (hill); *nui* (big). Big hill.

Pukengerengere *puke* (hill); *ngerengere* (leprosy or skin disease). Hill where a sufferer from leprosy was isolated.

Pukeokaoka *puke* (hill); *okaoka* (South Island form of *ongaonga*: nettle). Hill where the nettles grow.

Pukeone *puke* (hill); *one* (sand). Sandy-topped hill.

Pukeowara *puke* (hill); *o* (of); *Wara* (Ward). Named after Sir Joseph Ward.

Pukepoto Dark blue earth used as a pigment. It is found in the nearby swamp.

Pukerau *puke* (hill); *rau* (many). Many hills.

Pukerauaruhe *puke* (hill or mound); *rau* (many); *aruhe* (fern-root). A great heap of fern-root.

Pukerangi *puke* (hill); *rangi* (sky). Hill that reaches up into the sky.

Pukerimu *puke* (hill); *rimu* (native tree). Rimu hill.

Pukeroa *puke* (hill); *roa* (long). Long hill.

Pukerua *puke* (hill); *rua* (two). Two hills.

Puketā *puke* (hill); *tā* (sloping). Sloping hill. Possibly a corruption of peketa (dart).

Puketai Literally, *puke* (hill); *tai* (sea). Hill beside the water. Puketai, which is the site of Andersons Bay, Dunedin, should be Puketahi, The first hill, i.e., the first of a series of hills down the Otago Peninsula.

Puketapu *puke* (hill); *tapu* (sacred). Sacred or forbidden hill.

Puketarata *puke* (hill); *tarata* (native tree). Lemonwood tree hill.

Puketawai *puke* (hill); *tawai* (native tree). Tawai hill.

Puketeraki *puke* (hill); *te* (the); *raki* (South Island form of *rangi*: sky). Hill reaching up to the sky. The proper form of the name is Puketiraki, tiraki meaning lifting sharply skywards.

Puketihi *puke* (hill); *tihi* (top). Top of the hill. From this peak the three mountains of the Tongariro National Park are seen on a clear day.

Puketiro *puke* (hill); *tiro* (view). Hill with an extensive view from the summit.

Puketitiro *puke* (hill); *titiro* (view). Hill with a commanding view.

Puketoi *puke* (hill); *toi* (summit). Summit of the hill.

Puketona *puke* (hill); *tona* (mound).

Puketōtara *puke* (hill); *tōtara* (native tree). Tōtara hill.

Puketūī *puke* (hill); *tūī* (native bird). Tūī hill.

Puketutu *puke* (hill); *tutu* (native tree). Tutu hill. There are several places of this name, and in some, as in Weeks Island, tutu is the tree; in others it is a plant.

Pukeuri Named after a woman on the Ārai-te-uru canoe. Literally, *puke* (hill); *uri* (dark). Dark hill.

Pukewāhia Firewood hill. Literally, *puke* (hill); *wāhia* (split, or divided). Split hill.

Pukewhero *puke* (hill); *whero* (red). Red hill. Named by a party in 1932 because the last few hundred feet are a jumble of bright-red rocks.

Pūkorokio A bunch of koromiko. It is said that here, near Riverton, moa were killed. Koromiko was the wood traditionally used for cooking moa. The stream of this name in Central Otago is now called Moa Creek.

Puku Named after a woman carried away by the māeroero. Literally, belly.

Pukurahi *puku* (belly); *rahi* (big). Big belly.

Pukutahi Named for a chief who was killed at Lake Te Anau. Literally, *puku* (belly); *tahi* (single).

Punakāiki *puna* (a spring); *kāiki* (a misspelling of *kāike* or *kāika*: to lie in a heap). This is the site of the famous pancake rocks, which lie in heaps, and the 'spring' is no doubt the blow-hole. But there was a Ngāi Tahu belief that Punakāiki is a word that describes the neck and throat of a human being, the rock and blow-holes being likened to them.

Punakītere Swiftly flowing spring.

Punapito *puna* (spring); *pito* (end). End of the spring.

Punaruku *puna* (spring); *ruku* (to sink or dive). To sink into a spring. The name has been brought from Hawaiki.

Puni The encampment, or to be blocked up.

Pūniho Ambush.

Pūniu Fern.

Puniwhakaū *puni* (camp); *whakaū* (to arrive). To reach camp.

Punganui A corrupt form of Ponganui, a large tree-fern.

Pungarehu Ashes.

Pūponga Hunched up.

Pupū The largest freshwater spring in New Zealand at Tākaka was for years misnamed. The name's origin has been widely debated. Properly it was known to Māori as Waikaremūmū (silent waters), which could be rendered Boisterous wind that ruffled the waters. It was shortened by Pākehā to Mumu, and possibly corrupted to Bubu; but the Bubu diggings were some miles away. The name was given to the springs, and it was thought that the original Māori name must have been Pupū. Now officially known as Waikoropupū Springs.

The Pūpū Stream in Marlborough is named after a shellfish.

Pupuke The name in full is Pupukemoana, the overflowing lake.

Pūrakanui Correctly, Pūrākaunui. *Pū* (heap); *rākau* (timber); *nui* (big). Big heap of firewood. The inhabitants of Goat Island were slaughtered in tribal warfare and their bodies put in a great pile like a heap of firewood. Alternatively, *puraka* (crayfish basket); *nui* (big).

Puramāhoi *pura* (to twinkle or shine); *māhoi* (steadily). To shine steadily.

Pūrangi A bag net for catching lampreys. Such nets were totally enclosed except for a narrow opening, and this place was a clearing in the bush with a similar appearance.

Pūrau A spear or fork. It may have had some connection with a traditional mussel basket.

Pūrēhua A moth.

Pūrekireki Tufts of grass, or a heap of fragments.

Pureora A sacred rite performed for the recovery of the sick.

Purerua *pure* (to set free from tapu); *rua* (two).

Pūrewa To float.

Pūriri Native tree. The place was named because the pūriri grew so plentifully.

Puru Full, or a plug.

Putangahau Possibly a shortened form of Te Putanga-o-te-hau, the place where the wind comes from.

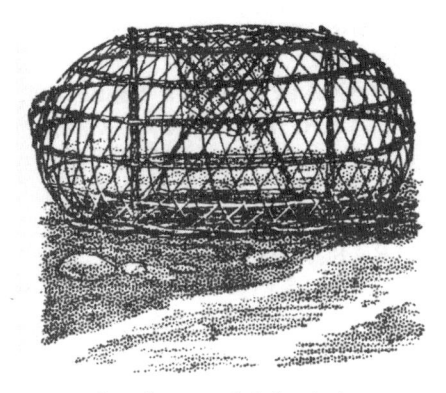

Puraka: crayfish basket

Putarepo The place at the end of the swamp where it could be crossed.

Pūtaringamotu The place of the severed ear. It was a figurative expression for the isolated remnant of kahikatea floodplain forest in west Christchurch, and known as either Riccarton Bush or Deans Bush.

Putāruru Correctly, Putaāruru. *Puta* (hole, or to appear); *ā* (after the manner of); *ruru* (owl, or morepork). The nest or hole of a morepork, which is often found in a hollow tree.

Pūtiki In full, Pūtiki-wharanui-a-Tamatea-pōkai-whenua, the place where Tamatea the navigator tied his topknot with flax. Tamatea of the Tākitimu canoe went ashore at Whanganui and had his hair dressed. The slave procured flax, but it was rotten and broke. Tamatea said it was not like the wharanui (a kind of flax) obtained on the East Coast. The place was named after the incident.

Pūtōrino Flute.

Pūwera Warm.

Pūtōrino: flute

Raetihi *rae* (headland); *tihi* (summit). Prominent summit.

Rāhiri To welcome.

Rāhotu *rā* (sun); *hotu* (to long for). To long for the sun.

Rāhui Boundary post. In full, Pourāhui. It also means a sanctuary.

Rai Ribbed, or furrowed. It probably should be *rae* (headland).

Rākaia Arrange in ranks. It is the South Island form of *rāngaia* (to arrange in ranks), and refers to the need for strong men to stand in ranks to break the force of the current for the weaker ones when attempting to ford the river.

Rakanui Correctly, Rākaunui. *Rākau* (tree); *nui* (big). Big tree.

Rākau Tree, or timber.

Rākauhauka *rākau* (wood, or tree); *hauka* (South Island form of *haunga*: to stink).

Rākauhaunga See Rakauhauka.

Rākaumangamanga *rākau* (wood, or tree); *mangamanga* (puzzling, mystical). The full name for Cape Brett is Rākaumangamanga-mai-ki-Hawaiki, an ancient name itself brought from Hawaiki.

Rākaunui *rākau* (tree); *nui* (big, or many). Big tree, or many trees.

Rākauroa *rākau* (tree); *roa* (long). Tall tree.

Rākautao *rākau* (timber); *tao* (spear). Wood for making spears.

Rakiura *raki* (South Island form of *rangi*: sky); *ura* (glowing). Glowing sky. The Māori name for Stewart Island. There is another tale that a young chief wished to marry but arrived just too late, for the young woman had already wed. The name in full is Te Ura-o-Te-Rakitāmau, The blushing of Te Rakitāmau.

Ramahiku Māori form of Damascus.

Ramarama A native tree.

Rānana Māori form of London.

Rānui *rā* (sun); *nui* (many). Plenty of sunshine. A modern name.

Ranganui *ranga* (parade); *nui* (big). A long line of warriors.

Rangataua A grasshopper; or *ranga* (line of warriors); *taua* (war party). Warriors drawn up in ranks.

Rangatira Chief.

Rangaunu *ranga* (shoal of fish); *unu* (to pull out). Good fishing.

Rangiahua Great; or to approach the sky.

Rangiaowhia *rangi* (sky); *aowhia* (clouded). Clouded sky.

Rangiātea Short for Rangiātea-te-tūāhu-o-Io-mata-kanakana, the shrine of Io of the far-seeing eyes. A name that came from Hawaiki (it is the Māori name for Ra'iatea, the sacred island in the Society Islands).

Rangihaeata The first rays of morning light.

Rangiawhia See Rangiaowhia.

Rangihoua Named after a chief of long ago.

Rangikura *rangi* (sky); *kura* (red). Red sky. The original name was Whenuakura, red land.

Rangiora Good weather after a bad spell, or an invalid getting better, or day of peace. In the North Island it refers to a shrub (bushman's friend).

Rangiotū The day of the god of war.

Rangipō *rangi* (sky); *pō* (night). The place where the sky is dark, a reference to the time when Ngātoroirangi called down fire on his enemies.

Rangiputa *rangi* (sky); *puta* (to pass through). To cross the sky.

Rangiriri *rangi* (sky); *riri* (angry). The angry sky.

Rangitaikī *rangi* (chief); *tai* (tide); *kī* (full). A great river like a full tide.

Rangitata *rangi* (sky, or day); *tata* (lowering clouds). A day of lowering clouds.

Rangitīkei *rangi* (sky, or day); *tīkei* (to stretch the legs). The day of striding out. It may also refer to a ford that was crossed by walking on tip-toes.

Rangitoto *rangi* (sky, or day); *toto* (blood). A common name in New Zealand, usually imported from Hawaiki. Rangitoto Island, Auckland, is in full Ngā Rangi-i-totongia-a-Tamatekapua, the days of the bleeding of Tamatekapua. The famous chief of the Arawa canoe was badly wounded here.

Rangitūkia *rangi* (day); *tūkia* (to be attacked). The day of the attack.

Rangiuru *rangi* (sky); *uru* (west). The western sky.

Rangiwāhia *rangi* (sky); *wāhia* (to split). Gap through which the sky can be seen, or a glimpse of heaven. A party of travellers came either to a clearing, or to a moment when there was a rift in the clouds.

Raorikia Māori form of Laodicea.

Rapahoe Paddle blade.

Rāpaki Kilt. When the chief Te Rangiwhakaputa took possession, he put down his kilt to mark his ownership.

Rapaura Running waters.

Rāroa *rā* (day); *roa* (long). Named by Īhenga because he spent so many hours paddling his canoe.

Rātā A native tree.

Rātana Named after the prophet Tahupōtiki Wiremu Rātana.

Rātānui *rātā* (native tree); *nui* (many). Plenty of rātā trees.

Arawa canoe

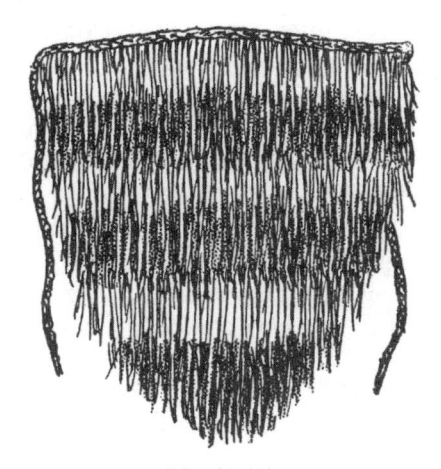

Rāpaki: kilt

Raukawa Leaves of kawakawa. They were worn by a chief in mourning and gave the name of the Ngāti Raukawa tribe. Raukawa Moana is the Māori name for Cook Strait.
Raukūmara *rau* (leaf); *kūmara* (sweet potato). Kūmara leaves.
Raumati Summer.
Raupō Native reed.
Raurimu *rau* (many, or leaf); *rimu* (red pine). Many rimu or Rimu leaf.
Rāwene *rā* (day); *wene* (many). Many days.
Rāwhiti The place of the sunrise.
Rāwhitiroa *rā* (sun); *whiti* (to shine); *roa* (long). Long sunshine. It may also mean In the direct line of the sun, as the settlement ran from east to west.

Rēhia Pleasure.
Rehutai Sea spray.
Reikorangi The gate of heaven, or the breast of heaven. A slave of this name was buried here.
Rēinga The underworld.
Rēkohu *rē* (see); *kohu* (mist; or possibly a personal name). The name for Pitt Island is now applied to the whole Chatham Islands.
Remuera Correctly, Remuwera, the burnt edge of a flax garment; or Burnt buttocks, a reference to a cannibal feast.
Repo Swamp.
Reporoa *repo* (swamp); *roa* (long). Long swamp.
Rere Waterfall.
Retāruke Correctly, reretāruke. *Rere* (waterfall); *tāruke* (trap for crayfish).
Rewa To begin, or to meet.
Rewanui *rewa* (mast); *nui* (big). Big mast.
Rewarewa Native tree.
Rikiriki Scattered.
Rimu Red pine.
Rimunui *rimu* (red pine); *nui* (big, or many). Many rimu.
Rimurapa *rimu* (seaweed); *rapa* (to look for). The Māori name for Sinclair Head.
Rimutaka Correctly, Remutaka, to sit down to rest. It refers to an

Rīpa   Rotokākahi

incident when Hau was pursuing his wife.

Rīpa Correctly, Rīpapa. *Rī* (flax rope); *papa* (flat rock). A canoe was tied by a flax rope to a rock on the island.

Riponui *ripo* (whirlpool); *nui* (big). Big whirlpool.

Riwaka Correctly, Riuwaka. *Riu* (inside, or bulge); *waka* (canoe). The inside or bulge of a canoe.

Rohepōtae *rohe* (rim or space enclosed); *pōtae* (hat). Rim of the hat, or space enclosed by the hat, the term applied to the King Country after the New Zealand Wars.

Romahapa *roma* (stream, or channel); *hapa* (crooked). Crooked channel.

Rona To bind, or swirling.

Rongokōkako *rongo* (to listen); *kōkako* (native crow). Listening to the kōkako. It may be named after the father of Tamatea.

Rongotai *rongo* (sound); *tai* (sea). The sound of the sea. A modern name.

Rongotea Probably named after a chief.

Roto Lake.

Rotoaira *roto* (lake); *a* (of); *Ira* (a person). The lake of Ira.

Rotoakiwa *roto* (lake); *a* (of); *Kiwa* (a person). The lake of Kiwa.

Rotoatara *roto* (lake); *a* (of); *Tara* (a chief). The lake of Tara, who killed the taniwha that inhabited it. The lake is now dried up.

Rotoatua *roto* (lake); *atua* (god). The lake of the god.

Rotoehu *roto* (lake); *ehu* (turbid). Turbid lake.

Rotoiti *roto* (lake); *iti* (little). Little lake. The full name of the northern Rotoiti was Te Roto-iti-kite-ā-Īhenga-i-ariki-ai-Kahu, the little lake seen or discovered by Īhenga that gave chiefly status to Kahumatamomoe.

Rotokaha *roto* (lake); *kaha* (boundary). The boundary lake.

Rotokākahi *roto* (lake); *kākahi* (freshwater shellfish). The shellfish were killed by the Tarawera eruption. The Green Lake.

Raupō: New Zealand reed

Rotokawa *roto* (lake); *kawa* (bitter). Lake of bitter waters.

Rotokawau *roto* (lake); *kawau* (shag). Shag lake.

Rotokohu *roto* (lake); *kohu* (fog or mist). Misty lake.

Rotomā *roto* (lake); *mā* (clear). Lake of clear waters.

Rotomahana *roto* (lake); *mahana* (warm). Warm lake.

Rotomakariri *roto* (lake); *makariri* (cold). Cold lake.

Rotomanu *roto* (lake); *manu* (bird). Lake of birds.

Rotongaro *roto* (lake); *ngaro* (lost, or hidden). Hidden lake.

Rotoroa *roto* (lake); *roa* (long). Long lake.

Rotorua *roto* (lake); *rua* (two). The second lake. The full name was Te Rotorua-nui-a-Kahumatamomoe. It was the second big lake to be discovered by Īhenga, who named it after his father-in-law Kahumatamomoe.

Rototuna *roto* (lake); *tuna* (eel). Eel lake.

Rotowaro *roto* (lake); *waro* (live coals). A fire glowing by the lakeside.

Rotowhero *roto* (lake); *whero* (red). Red lake, so called because of the oxide of iron deposits.

Rotowhio *roto* (lake); *whio* (blue duck). Lake or pool of the blue duck.

Rotu A sleep-making spell.

Ruahine A wise woman, or an old woman.

Ruakākā Nesting place of the parakeets.

Ruakituri *ruaki* (to vomit); *turi* (knee, or post).

Ruakura *rua* (pit); *kura* (red). Pit in the red earth.

Ruakurī *rua* (pit); *kurī* (dog). Cave of the dogs. Wild dogs were found living by the mouth of the cave.

Ruamāhanga *rua* (two); *māhanga* (fork). Twin forks. Hau discovered a drinking trough and a bird-snare in the twin forks of a tree.

Ruamoko *rua* (pit or hole); *moko* (lizard). Home of the lizard.

Ruapehu *rua* (hole); *pehu* (to explode, or make a loud noise). Ruapehu has two vents or blow-holes from which steam is expelled. An alternative is Ruapahū. *Rua* (pit); *pahū* (to resound), a reference to the violent explosions heard during eruptions on the mountain.

Ruapekapeka *rua* (hole);

pekapeka (native bat). The bat's nest. Thousands of bats lived in tree hollows here.

Ruapuke   *rua* (two); *puke* (hill). Two hills.

Ruaroa   *rua* (pit); *roa* (long). Long pit.

Ruatāhuna   *rua* (two, or pit); *tāhuna* (sandbank). Two sandbanks.

Ruataniwha   *rua* (two); *taniwha* (water-monster). Two great taniwha once lived in the lake. They fought over a boy who fell in, and their struggles formed the Tukituki and Waipawa rivers, which drained the lake. Other places with this name mean Taniwha pit or cave.

Ruatangata   *rua* (pit); *tangata* (man). Cave in which people lived.

Ruatapu   *rua* (pit); *tapu* (sacred). Sacred cave.

Ruatoki   *rua* (pit, or two); *toki* (adze). Two adzes, or adze in the cave.

Ruatōria   Correctly, Rua-a-Tōria, kūmara pit belonging to the chief Tōria.

Ruawāhia   *rua* (pit); *wāhia* (split). Gulch cleft by volcanic action.

Ruawai   *rua* (pit, or two); *wai* (water). Water in a cave, or two streams.

Ruawaro   *rua* (cave); *waro* (live coals). Embers in a cave.

Rukuhia   Gathered together, or dived for.

Rūnanga   An assembly.

Runaruna   A plant, or a game.

Ruru   Owl or morepork.

T

Taemaro   *tae* (to dye); *maro* (apron). Dyed apron.

Tahaia   *taha* (to pass, on one side); *ia* (current). Passing along the slack water of the stream.

Tahakopa   *taha* (side); *kopa* (curved). Curved side.

Tahatika   Coastline, or at the edge of the river.

Tahawai   *taha* (side); *wai* (sea). Seaside.

Tāheke   Waterfall.

Tāhekeaua   *tāheke* (waterfall); *aua* (herring). A place for catching herrings by the waterfall.

Tāhekeroa   Long river rapid or cataract.

Tahora   A clearing, or an expanse of open country.

Tahoraiti Small clearing.

Tahoramaurea Uncultivated, or covered with tussocks.

Tāhuna Sandbank or shoal.

Tāhunanui *tāhuna* (sandbank); *nui* (large).

Tāhurangi The first man to ascend Taranaki (Mount Egmont). Literally, *tāhu* (ridgepole); *rangi* (sky).

Taiamai An old name for the Bay of Islands. It is embodied in the saying Ka kata ngā pūriri o Taiamai, the pūriri trees of Taiamai are laughing.

Taiaroa Named after the chief Taiaroa.

Taieri Correctly, Taiari, tide on the eleventh night of the moon.

Taihape Originally Ōtaihape, the place of Taihape. Literally, *tai* (angle); *hape* (crooked).

Taiharuru *tai* (sea); *haruru* (resounding). Thundering sea.

Taihoa By and by.

Tāikirau *tāiki* (snag); *rau* (many). Many snags.

Tāiko The name of a Māori man, sometimes spelt Tycho. Literally, rib or basket.

Taikōrea *tai* (sea); *kōrea* (small canoe). Small canoe on the sea.

Tainui One of the canoes of the migration. Literally, *tai* (sea); *nui* (big). Great sea.

Taioma White soil.

Taipo Goblin, or devil. The river was given this name because when it was in flood it deserved the name. It is no doubt of modern origin.

Taipoiti Little Taipo.

Taipuha A very high tide.

Tairāwhiti *tai* (tide); *rā* (sun) *whiti* (shining, eastern). The East Coast and Gisborne area is known as the Coast of shining sun or The coast on which the sun shines across the water.

Tairua *tai* (tide); *rua* (two). Two tides, one from the north and the other from the south.

Taitā Driftwood in the bed of the river.

Taitamāhine *tai* (sea); *tamāhine* (girls). Also **Te Tai Tamāhine**. The sea of girls — the peaceful east coast waters of the northern North Island, compared with Taitamatāne, the rough west coast, which was called the sea of men, where warriors were needed to man the canoes.

Taitamatāne Also **Te Tai Tamatane**. See Taitamāhine.

Taitapu An obsolete word for

boundary. Literally, *tai* (tide); *tapu* (sacred).

Taitimu *tai* (tide); *timu* (ebb). Ebb tide.

Tai Hauāuru *tai* (coast); *hauāuru* (western).

Tai-o-Aorere *tai* (coast); *o* (of); *Aorere* (flying foam). The Māori name for the Nelson and Tasman Bay coast.

Tai-o-Ārai-te-uru *tai* (coast); *o* (of); *Ārai-te-uru* (the voyaging canoe). The coast of South Otago and eastern Southland.

Tai-o-Marokura *tai* (coast); *o* (of); *Marokura* (a deity). The waters off North Canterbury and Marlborough, particularly the Kaikōura area.

Tai-o-Mahaanui *tai* (coast); *o* (of); *Mahaanui* (the canoe of Māui). The waters off Canterbury and Otago.

Tai-o-Rēhua *tai* (coast); *o* (of); *Rēhua* (a deity). The Tasman Sea. Often Te Tai-o-Rēhua.

Tai Poutini *tai* (coast); *Poutini* (an embodiment of greenstone). The West Coast. See Poutini.

Tai Tapu *tai* (coast); *tapu* (sacred). A name for Golden Bay.

Tai Tokerau *tai* (coast); *tokerau* (north). Northland.

Takahanga Track or footpath.

Takahē Native bird, the Notornis.

Takahiwai *takahi* (to tramp); *wai* (water). To trample into the water.

Takahue *taka* (heap); *hue* (gourd). Heap of gourds.

Tākaka Bracken. A name that comes from the Society Islands.

Takānini Named after the nineteenth-century chief Ihaka Takaanini.

Takapau Flax sleeping mat. A pā in the far north was given this name because the people of Tainui put down a mat and went to sleep, i.e., they resided there for some time.

Tākapu Gannet.

Takapuna *taka* (assembly); *puna* (spring). The gathering of people who drank at the spring were Tainui men claiming possession of the land.

Tākāiritawa To jerk out of the water. Thousands of ducks were caught in this way.

Takiroa *taki* (Southern version of *tangi*, sound); *roa* (long). Echo. The name of the rock shelter at Waitaki where there are ancient paintings. There is a very clear echo.

Tākitimu A famous canoe of the migration commanded by

Tamatea. It was petrified in the form of the Tākitimu Mountains (previously spelt Takitimo).

Takitūī *taki* (to follow); *tūī* (native bird). To follow the tūī.

Takiwā-waiariki *takiwā* (district); *waiariki* (hot springs). A general name for the central North Island thermal district.

Takutai *taku* (coast); *tai* (sea). Sea coast.

Tama-ahua The peak on Mount Taranaki is named after the first Māori to ascend it.

Tamahere *tama* (son); *here* (tie up).

Tāmaki Battle, omen. The Auckland isthmus was Tāmaki-whenua, a contested land.

Tāmaki-makaurau Tāmaki of a hundred lovers. The Māori name for Auckland.

Tamarau *tama* (son); *rau* (many). Many sons.

Tamatea Honouring the great navigator Tamatea-pōkai-whenua, this is the Māori name for Dusky Sound.

Tāneatua The name commemorates the tohunga (navigator, priest) of the Mataatua canoe.

Tāneauroa Named after an old chief. Literally, *tāne* (man); *au* (whirlpool); *roa* (long). The man of the long rapid or whirlpool.

Tānekaha *tāne* (man); *kaha* (strong). Strong man.

Taniwha Monster.

Tangiihi Correctly, Tangaehe, the noise of the rustling or murmuring tide. There are beds of shells on the foreshore and the waves ripple over them.

Tangahoe Named by Turi after his paddle.

Tangarākau Fallen trees, referring to a great quantity of trees carried down by the river when in flood.

Tangiaro In full, Tangi-aro-o-Kahu. *Tangi* (to weep); *aro* (desire for); *o* (of); *Kahu* (Kahumatamomoe). After the death of his father, Kahumatamomoe turned his face to Moehau where his father was buried, and chanted a lament of yearning and sorrow.

Tangimoana *tangi* (lament); *moana* (ocean). The lament of the ocean.

Tangitere *tangi* (to cry or lament); *tere* (swiftly, or to float).

Tangiterōria *tangi* (to cry); *te* (the); *rōria* (conch shell). The sound of the trumpet. Eel weirs were built on the Wairoa River, and as the Māori paddled their canoes up to them the force of the water was audible and was likened to the sound of a conch shell being blown.

Tangiwai *tangi* (to weep or lament); *wai* (water). Weeping waters. Noted for its sudden floods, which many years ago were responsible for the death of a chief, and for the terrible railway disaster in 1953. Fiordland greenstone is called tangiwai because of the flecks in it that resemble tears.

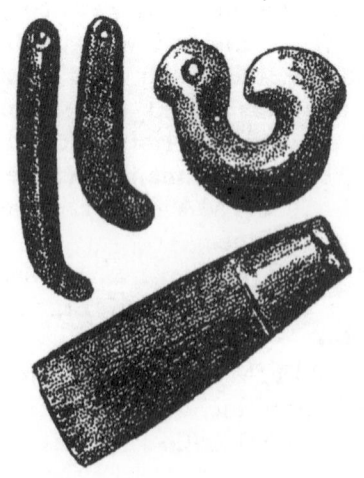

Tangiwai: a type of greenstone

Tangoio *tango* (to take hold of); *io* (a strand of rope or lock of hair). To hold a strand of rope. The name may be that of a chief.

Tangowahine *tango* (to seize); *wahine* (woman). To abduct a woman.

Taonui *tao* (spear); *nui* (big). Great spear.

Taoroa *tao* (spear); *roa* (long). Long spear.

Tapanui Possibly a contraction of Te-tapuae-o-Uenuku, the footprints of the rainbow god. Or literally, the great edge, referring to the edge of the forest. A third theory is that the name was originally Te Papanui, the great flat area of country.

Tapawera *tapa* (edge); *wera* (hot, or burnt). The burnt fringe (of the forest).

Tapu Sacred. Usually given for a particular reason, as at Coromandel, where a great battle resulted in many dead being buried and making the place sacred; or as at Riwaka, where a (priest, expert) placed a hair of his head near the doorway of his house to keep intruders away.

Tapuaeharuru *tapuae* (footsteps); *haruru* (resounding). The noise of footsteps, or resounding footsteps. At Taupō the name was given because of the caverns that caused footsteps to resound. Īhenga gave the name in Northland because of his own footsteps.

Tapuae-o-Uenuku *tapuae* (footsteps); *o* (of); *Uenuku* (the rainbow god). The footsteps of the rainbow god. The mountain was previously Mount Tapuaenuku. It was possibly named after a chief called Tapuaenuku.

Tapuhi To nurse.

Tāpui Friend, or close companion.

Tapuwae Footsteps, the place in Taranaki named by Turi. Tapuwae, site of the Wairoa Post Office, was named by Sir James Carroll after a chief.

Tapuwaeharuru See Tapuaeharuru.

Tapuwaeroa *tapuwae* (footsteps); *roa* (long). Long footsteps. They were made by the giant Rongokako, who left his footprints at Cape Kidnappers, Māhia, and East Cape.

Tarakai *tara* (seabird); *kai* (to live). A place where sea birds nested.

Tarakohe *tara* (thorn); *kohe* (native plant).

Taramakau Possibly Teremakau. *Tere* (to flow); *makau* (curve). Another interpretation is that it means *tere* (swift); *makau* (spouse), referring to a man who was in search of his absconding wife who turned to stone.

Taramea Spear-grass.

Taranaki There have been many theories about this name. *Tara* (peak), presents no problems; *naki* may be *ngaki* (clear of vegetation). Probably Taranaki was the tribal name given to the mountain. A very old name for the mountain was Pukehaupapa, ice mountain, and when referring to its graceful shape it was called Puke-o-Naki, *puke* (hill, or pubic area); *o* (of); *Naki* (a female ancestor).

Tararua *tara* (peak); rua (two). Two peaks. The double peaks of the Tararua Range opposite Ōtaki are Pukeamoamo and Pukeahurangi, both named by Rangikaikore (Rangi the foodless), because he broke two tara or bird spears while on the range.

Tarata A native tree.

Taratahi *tara* (peak); *tahi* (single). Single peak — in this case Mount Holdsworth.

Tarawera *tara* (bird spear); *wera* (burnt). Hikawera of Hawke's Bay had a successful season killing birds, and left his spears in a hut. When he returned the next season

Tāreha

he found that the hut and his spears had been burnt.

Tāreha Ochre.

Tārewa The full name is Tārewapounamu. *Tārewa* (to suspend); *pounamu* (greenstone). A greenstone ornament was hung on a tree as a sacred offering.

Tāriki Possibly Tārika, to toss about.

Taringamotu *taringa* (ear); *motu* or *mutu* (cut off). Mutilated ear. See Pūtaringamotu.

Tārukenga Place of slaughter.

Tātaikoko *tātai* (to adorn); *koko* (pendant). The chief Pawa adorned himself at this place.

Tātara-a-kina *tātara* (spine); *a* (of); *kina* (sea urchin). The spines of the sea urchin. An old chief of Taupō compared this mountainous country to the sea urchins of Heretaunga.

Tātaramoa Bush lawyer (plant), or a type of fish.

Tatara A species of mollusc or fish.

Tatū To be content, or to touch bottom.

Tātuanui *tātua* (girdle); *nui* (big). Large girdle.

Taueru Hanging in clusters.

Tauhara Isolated, alone. The mountain stands alone on the plain.

Tauherenīkau Correctly, Tauwharenīkau, the over-hanging nīkau palms. When Hau was travelling in the Wairarapa he discovered a whare whose walls and roof were thatched with nīkau leaves.

Tauhoa To befriend.

Taukitua The further ridge.

Taumarere To fall, or **Taumārere**: a cord passed over the ridgepole of a house. Possibly Taumāriri, tranquil season.

Taumarunui *taumaru* (screen); *nui* (big). Huge screen. When the chief Pēhi Tāroa was dying, he asked that a screen be erected to shade him from the sun. He died before the work was completed with the words 'taumaru nui' on his lips.

Taumata Brow of a hill. This is a component of many place names.

Taumatawhakatangihangakōauauotamateapōkaiwhenuakitanatahu The brow of the hill where Tamatea who sailed all round the land played his nose flute to his beloved. The chief and explorer Tamatea-pōkaiwhenua here played a lament for his brother, who had been killed in a battle with Ngāti Hine.

There are several forms of this firmly established Māori name, the longest in the country if not in the world. One, broken into its component parts, is Te Taumata-okiokinga-whakatangihanga-o-te-kōauau-a-Tamatea-pōkai-whenua. The sign at this location near Porangahau lists the extended, 84-letter version using a Taumatawhakatangihanga-koauaotamateaturipūkakapiki-maungahoronukupōkaiwhenua-kitanatahu; this adds a description of Tamatea as 'the chief of great physical stature and renown'.

Tauoma Short for Tauomaoma, to race, strive in running; or a race.

Taupaki A loin mat; or a season of fine weather.

Tauparikākā Correctly, Tauparekākā; *taupare* (to blindfold); *kākā* (parrot). To blindfold a parrot. This was done to decoy kākā, which were fairly tame. It prevented them from flying away.

Taupiri *tau* (ridge of hill); *piri* (to keep close to). It has been rendered, To clasp round the waist.

Taupō Short for Taupō-nui-a-Tia. *Taupō* (shoulder-cloak); *nui* (big); *a* (of); *Tia* (the discoverer of the lake). The great cloak of Tia. It is said Tia gave the name at lakeside upon seeing a cliff that resembled his flax cloak. Tia slept by the lake, and it has been conjectured that Taupō is a reference to his long sleep at night at that place.

Tauranga A sheltered anchorage, or a resting place for canoes.

Tauranga: canoe anchorage

Taurangakawau *tauranga* (sheltered place); *kawau* (shag). A roosting place for shags.

Taurangakohu *tauranga* (resting place); *kohu* (mists). A place where mists linger.

Taurangamangō *tauranga* (landing place); *mangō* (shark). Where the sharks were landed.

An old name for Shelly Beach in Auckland.

Tauraroa *taura* (rope); *roa* (long). Long rope.

Taurarua *taura* (rope); *rua* (two). Two ropes. The Māori name for Judges Bay.

Taurewa Having no settled home.

Tauriko A Pākehā-given name. Originally Taurico, standing for Tauranga Rimu Company. It was thought to be a misspelt Māori name and changed to Tauriko.

Taurikura *tauri* (feather ornament); *kura* (red). Ornament of red feathers.

Tautāne *tau* (ridge of a hill); *tāne* (man). Man on the ridge.

Tautoro To stretch forward.

Tautuku To stoop, or to be at a loss.

Tauwharanui *tau* (ridge of a hill); *wharanui* (a species of flax). Flax bushes on the ridge.

Tauwhare To overhang, or a shelter.

Tawa A native tree.

Tawanui *tawa* (tree); *nui* (many). Plenty of tawa trees.

Tāwirikohukohu Whirling mists. The mountain holds the clouds when the rest of the Tararua Range is clear.

Tawhai A native tree.

Tāwharanui *tāwhara* (kiekie flowers); *nui* (many). Plenty of kiekie flowers.

Tāwhiti Trap. This was a place where Pawa of the Bay of Plenty set a trap to catch Rongokako, the giant of Kahuranaki.

Tawhiti is a component of many place names. It is an allusion to Tahiti, and was brought from the Pacific homeland of the Māori people.

Tawhitinui An ancient name of great significance to Māori. It means Great Tahiti, in reference to the ancestral homeland.

Tāwhiuau Swirling mists.

Te Ahi-a-Manono The flames of Manono. The site of part of Lower Hutt, and a name of great antiquity, as it was a description of the burning of a great house on Manono.

Te Ahi-kai-kōura-a-Tama-ki-te-rangi The full name of Kaikōura.

Te Ahi-manawa-a-Te-Kohipipi The full name of the Ahimanawa Range.

Te Ahi-pūpū-a-Īhenga *te* (the); *ahi* (fire); *pūpū* (mussel); *a* (of); *Īhenga* (the explorer). The fire at which Īhenga cooked mussels.

Te Ahuahu *te* (the); *ahuahu* (mounds on which kūmara were grown).

Te Ākau *te* (the); *ākau* (rocky coast). The name was given by the tohunga (priest, expert) of the Tainui canoe because it was too rough to land here.

Te Ako-o-te-tūī-a-Tamaoho
The teaching of Tamaoho's tūī (bird). It was by a waterfall on the Whangamarino Stream. Tūī were taught to speak, usually by a waterfall where there was no other sound to disturb the sound of the teacher's voice.

Te Anahāwea *te* (the); *ana* (cave); *Hāwea* (the Hāwea tribe). Smoke was seen coming from this cave in Bligh Sound in 1842, but the inhabitants of the 'lost tribe' fled. Subsequently this name was applied to the sound.

Te Anahīnātore *te* (the); *ana* (cave); *hīnātore* (phosphorescent). This is the famous rediscovered glow-worm cave of Te Anau, named Te Ana-au.

Te Anau The full name is Te Ana-au, *te* (the); *ana* (cave); *au* (swirling), in reference to a glowworm cave on the lake. The name has no shortage of alternative explanations: to move to and fro as reeds in a lake; named after a Waitaha chieftainess; the rain on the water; the uneven surface; the long view; the lake of many arms; water current in a cave. Of these the most likely seems that it may have been named after Te Anau, the daughter of Hekeia.

Te Anga *te* (the); *anga* (cockle shell, or fruit stone).

Te Ara-a-Hongi Hongi's Track.

Te Ara-a-Kiwa The pathway of Kiwa. The Māori name for Foveaux Strait; Kiwa is a sea god.

Te Ārai *te* (the); *ārai* (screen).

Te Araroa *te* (the); *ara* (path); *roa* (long). The long path. The place near East Cape was named by Māori after the residence of a missionary who had a long path to the front of his house.

Te Arawhata The ladder or bridge. A ravine that gave access to the Panekiri Bluff, Waikaremoana.

Te Aro *te* (the); *aro* (face, or front).

Te Aroha *te* (the); *aroha* (love or affection). Kahumatamomoe sat on the summit of this mountain of love, and his heart was filled with affection for the land and people of Te Paeroa-o-Toi, the long range of Toi.

Te Atatū *te* (the); *atatū* (dawn).

Te Au The cloud or fog, the site of the Town Belt in Dunedin.

Te Aumiti *te* (the); *au* (current); *miti* (swallowed up). The Māori name for French Pass, which in legend was formed by a cormorant.

Te Aunui-o-tonga *te* (the); *au* (current); *nui* (great); *o* (of); *tonga* (south). The Manawatū Gorge through which the south winds blow.

Te Aute *te* (the); *aute* (paper mulberry tree). The name commemorates an unsuccessful attempt to grow this tropical tree, which is so important in other parts of Polynesia.

Te Awa *te* (the); *awa* (river, or channel).

Te Awaiti *te* (the); *awa* (river, or channel); *iti* (little). The little channel.

Te Awamutu *te* (the); *awa* (river); *mutu* (cut short, or ended). The river above this point was blocked by snags and was unsuitable for canoes.

Te Hana *te* (the); *hana* (glow).

Te Hāpara *te* (the); *hāpara* (spade).

Te Hāroto *te* (the); *hāroto* (pool).

Te Heuheu The body of a famous chief was buried near Lake Taupō, and it was difficult to find at a later date because of the brushwood that had grown over it. The high chief Tūkino had a son, who was named Te Heuheu from this event, and the highest peak of Mount Tongariro bears his name.

Te Hīnau *te* (the); *hīnau* (native tree).

Te Hoe Short for Te Hoe-o-Tainui. See Hoe-o-Tainui

Te Hoiere Named after a canoe, it is the Māori name for Pelorus Sound.

Te Hope *te* (the); *hope* (waist). This river crossing was waist deep.

Te Horo *te* (the); *horo* (landslide). A descriptive name.

Te Hūria *te* (the); *Hūria* (Māori form of Judea).

Te Ikaamaru *te* (the); *ika* (fish); *a* (of); *Maru*. It was once misspelt Te Kaminaru.

Te Ika-a-Māui *te* (the); *ika* (fish); *a* (of); *Māui* (the demigod). The Māori name for the North Island. It was the fish that Māui pulled up from the depths of the ocean.

Te Ika-a-Parehika The fish of Parehika. The Māori name of Lawyers Head, Dunedin, which legend says was a fish that Parehika pulled from the sea.

Te Ika-a-Poutini The fish of Poutini. An ancient name for the West Coast. Traditionally greenstone was the fish of Poutini, the taniwha (water spirit) who protected the West Coast.

Te Ika-a-Whataroa *te* (the); *ika* (fish); *a* (of); *whata* (storehouse); *roa* (long). The long fish storehouse or The fish of Whataroa. This is the correct form of Te Ikawhataroa, near Kaikōura.

Te Kaha *te* (the); *kaha* (rope, or boundary line).

Te Kairanga The place where much food is gathered. Forest, river and lagoon teemed with birds and fish, and the land was suitable for cultivation. The Māori name for Linton Military Camp.

Te Kākaho *te* (the); *kākaho* (toetoe or plume grass).

Te Kākāpō *te* (the); *kākāpō* (ground parrot). Kahu's dog caught a kākāpō here.

Te Kao *te* (the); *kao* (dried kūmara).

Tekapō Correctly, Takapō; *taka* (a floor mat); *pō* (night). An exploring party was surprised and frightened at night; they hastily rolled up their sleeping mats and made their departure.

Te Karaka *te* (the); *karaka* (native tree).

Te Kauanga-a-Hatupatu *te* (the); *kauanga* (swimming); *a* (of); *Hatupatu* (the young man who swam underwater from Rotorua to Mokoia Island).

Te Kaukaroa In full, Te Kaukaharoa. *Te* (the); *kaukaha* (to swim strongly); *roa* (long). The long, strong swimming of Hikaroa, who swam across lake Te Anau at its widest part.

Te Kauwhata *te* (the); *kau* (empty); *whata* (storehouse).

Te Kawa *te* (the); *kawa* (shrub).

Te Kawakawa *te* (the); *kawakawa* (shrub). The daughters of Kupe made a wreath of the leaves of kawakawa, and this place later became known as Cape Palliser. Several places with this name were remembered as place names from Hawaiki.

Te Kiri *te* (the); *kiri* (short for *kirikiri*: gravel).

Te Kiteroa *te* (the); *kite* (to see); *roa* (long). The long view.

Te Kōhakapouākai *te* (the); *kōhaka* (South Island form of *kōhanga*: nest); *pouākai* (fabulous gigantic bird).

Te Kōhanga *te* (the); *kōhanga* (nest).

Te Kopi *te* (the); *kopi* (meeting of streams).

Te Kōpuru *te* (the); *kopuru* (heavy clouds).

Te Kōroa *te* (the); *kōroa* (finger).

Te Kōura *te* (the); *kōura* (crayfish).

Te Kōwhai *te* (the); *kōwhai* (flowering tree).

Te Kūiti A contraction of Te Kūititanga, the narrowing in. A reference to the confiscation of Māori property after the Waikato War, and also to the constriction of the valley of the Mangaokewa Stream at this point.

Te Kūmara *te* (the); *kūmara* (sweet potato). The site of old kūmara plantations.

Te Kumi *te* (the); *kumi* (fabulous creature or monster).

Te Kupenga-a-Taramainuku *te* (the); *kupenga* (fishing net); *a* (of); *Taramainuku* (a chief). The islands at the entry to the Hauraki Gulf. Taramainuku cast his net across the gulf from Cape Colville to Whāngārei Heads. The Watchman was the centre post of the net, and the Hen and Chicken Islands the corks.

Te Kupenga-o-Kupe *te* (the); *kupenga* (fishing net); *o* (of); *Kupe* (the great explorer).

Te Kūrae-o-Tura The headland of Tura, the Māori name for the Devonport foreshore.

Te Kūraetanga-o-te-ihu-o-Hei *te* (the); *kūraetanga* (outward curve); *o* (of); *te* (the); *ihu* (nose); *o* (of); *Hei* (an explorer). The outward curve of Hei's nose, named by Hei as the Arawa canoe passed north to Hauraki. The island is sometimes known as The Chief's Nose.

Te Kurī-a-Pawa *te* (the); *kurī* (dog); *a* (of); *Pawa* (a famous Māori chief, aka Paoa). Later named Young Nick's Head by Captain Cook.

Te Māhia *te* (the); *māhia* (indistinct sound).

Te Māika *te* (the); *māika* (basket of cooked food).

Te Maire *te* (the); *maire* (native tree).

Te Mānia *te* (the); *mānia* (plain).

Te Māpara *te* (the); *māpara* (resin, or comb).

Te Mata *te* (the); *mata* (headland), and many other meanings.

Te Mataī *te* (the); *mataī* (native tree).

Te Matau-a-Māui The fish-hook of Māui, with which the North Island was hooked. The fish-hook is the great curve of Hawke Bay.

Te Maunga *te* (the); *maunga* (mountain).

Te Maungaroa *te* (the); *maunga* (mountain); *roa* (long).

Te Māwhai *te* (the); *māwhai* (parasitic plant).

Te Mira *te* (the); *mira* (Māori form of mill). A flour mill once stood here.

Te Miro *te* (the); *miro* (native tree).

Te Moana-nui-a-Kiwa See Moana-nui-a-Kiwa.

Te Motu-tapu-a-Tinirau *te* (the); *motu* (island); *tapu* (sacred); *a* (of); *Tinirau* (a legendary chief). The sacred island of Tinirau. An ancient name for Mokoia Island.

Te Namu *te* (the); *namu* (sandfly). Such names were usually given because of the presence of sandflies.

Te Ngae *te* (the); *ngae* (swamp).

Tengawai Probably a corruption of Te Anawai. *Te* (the); *ana* (cave); *wai* (water). The water cavern.

Te Ngāwhā *te* (the); *ngāwhā* (sulphurous springs). A descriptive name.

Te Ngutu-o-te-manu *te* (the); *ngutu* (beak); *o* (of); *te* (the); *manu* (bird). The beak of the bird.

Te Niho-o-te-kiore *te* (the); *niho* (tooth); *o* (of); *te* (the); *kiore* (rats). Rats' teeth. From an expression of Īhenga's wife when he brought home a bundle of rats and she saw their teeth.

Te Pahū *te* (the); *pahū* (gong). A stone or piece of wood that was struck to summon the people.

Te Paki *te* (the); *paki* (fine weather), and other meanings.

Te Papa *te* (the); *papa* (flat land). A descriptive name.

Te Papaioea Probably *te* (the); *papai* (good); *oea* (indeed). The Māori name for Palmerston North. See Papaioea.

Te Pāpapa *te* (the); *pāpapa* (calabash). At one time known locally as Pumpkin Flat. The Māori name, a rough translation of the English, was given by the local stationmaster when the railway line was extended here.

Te Papatapu *te* (the); *papa* (flat); *tapu* (sacred). The sacred flat.

Te Pari *te* (the); *pari* (precipice). A descriptive name for Sheerdown Mountain, Milford Sound.

Te Pēwhairangi See Pēowhairangi.

Te Pirita *te* (the); *pirita* (supplejack).

Te Pōhue *te* (the); *pōhue* (climbing plant such as convolvulus, clematis, etc.)

Poi: flax ball

Te Poi *te* (the); *poi* (ball).
Te Pokohiwi *te* (the); *pokohiwi* (shoulder). The Māori name for Boulder Bank.
Te Puapua-o-Hinenui-te-pō The entrance to the goddess of death. The fumerole that is now known as the Brain Pot at Whakarewarewa.
Te Puia Geyser, or hot spring.
Te Puka-a-Māui *te* (the); *puka* (South Island form of *punga*: anchor stone); *a* (of); *Māui* (the explorer). A Māori name for Stewart Island.
Te Puke *te* (the); *puke* (hill).
Te Puna *te* (the); *puna* (spring).
Te Puna-a-Tūhoe The springs of Tūhoe, the Māori name for Fairy Springs.
Te Puninga *te* (the); *puninga* (camping place).
Te Purotu Handsome, beautiful.

One old chief said to another, 'Te purotu o te wahine!' (What a beautiful wife you have!) and from this the place received its name.
Te Rā *te* (the); *rā* (sun). The Māori name for Daggs Sound, which opens up well to the sun.
Tērāpātiki *tērā* (that); *pātiki* (flounder, fish).
Te Rakipaewhenua *te* (the); *raki* (northern); *paewhenua* (expanse of land; dock or weed). The Māori name for the North Shore, Auckland.
Te Ramaroa *te* (the); *ramaroa* (eternal flame). Kupe navigated by this mountain to enter Hokianga Harbour.
Te Ranga-o-Taikehu *te* (the); *ranga* (sandspit); *o* (of); *Taikehu* (a member of the crew of Tainui who swam from this sandspit to the shore at Devonport). A fishing bank is also similarly named.
Te Rauamoa Probably Te Rauhamoa. *Te* (the); *rauhamoa* (extinct bird).
Te Rawa *te* (the); *rawa* (property, or the cause of a quarrel).
Terawhiti Correctly, Tarawhiti, near to the sunrise, or disturbed crossing.
Te Rēinga The leaping place of spirits. Wairua (souls) lowered

Te Rēinga: departing place of spirits

themselves from a branch of a pōhutukawa at Te Rēinga into the underworld below the kelp. The English name is Cape Rēinga.

Te Rere   *te* (the); *rere* (leap). Rere, rerenga, and rereka, all with the same meaning, are components of many place names, often recording famous leaps such as that of Hihi, who leaped hundreds of feet to escape his enemies. His fall was broken by trees, and the place named Te Rere-a-Hihi.

Te Rerenga Wairua   *te* (the); *rerenga* (leaping); *wairua* (soul). The leaping place of souls. See also Te Rēinga.

Te Rērewa   *te* (the); *rērewa* (Māori form of devil). A name given to a supposedly wicked man by missionary Māori.

Te Rore   *te* (the); *rore* (snare).

Te Roto   *te* (the); *roto* (lake). A component of many names.

Te Rou   *te* (the); *rou* (fowler). The name given because the postmaster was called Fowler.

Te Rua   *te* (the); *rua* (pit). A component of several names.

Te Ruahine   *te* (the); *ruahine* (old, or wise woman).

Te Tai   The coast. For various regional names such as Te Taitamāhine, Te Tai Tokerau, see Taitamāhine, Tai Tokerau, etc.

Te Tao-o-Kupe   The spear of Kupe. The Māori name for Jackson's Head where Kupe attempted to cast a spear across Cook Strait.

Te Tātua   *te* (the); *tātua* (girdle). Māori name for Three Kings, Auckland.

Te Tauihu o Te Waka   *te* (the); *tauihu* (bow figurehead); *o* (of); *te* (the); *waka* (canoe). A contemporary name for the north of the South Island. Traditionally the name extends to describe the canoe, either Te Waka-a-Aoraki or Te Waka-a-Māui.

Te Taumanu-o-Te-Waka-a-Māui   The thwart of Māui's canoe at Kaikōura.

Te Taumata   See Taumata.

Te Tawa *te* (the); *tawa* (native tree). At Te Tawa, Rotorua, Īhenga pushed his canoe with a piece of tawa wood. It stuck in the ground and he left it there, naming the place after it.

Te Teko *te* (the); *teko* (rock).

Te Tī *te* (the); *tī* (cabbage-tree).

Te Tipua *te* (the); *tipua* (goblin).

Te Tō *te* (the); *tō* (hauling-up place). The Māori name for Freeman's Bay, Auckland.

Te Tou-o-Te-Mātenga The sitting place of Marsden. A place where the Reverend Samuel Marsden sat to talk to Māori.

Te Tua *te* (the); *tua* (other side, or days gone by).

Te Tūāhu-a-Tuameke-te-ahi-tāpoa-i-taona-ai-te-manawa-o-Taiapua The sacred place of Tuameke, the smoky fire in which the heart of Taiapua was cooked. Between the Green and Blue lakes, Rotorua.

Te Uku *te* (the); *uku* (white clay).

Te Umu *te* (the); *umu* (oven). A component of many place names.

Te Upoko-o-Te-Ika *te* (the); *upoko* (head); *o* (of); *te* (the); *ika* (fish). The Wellington region is the head of the fish that Māui raised from the ocean.

Te Waewae *te* (the); *waewae* (leg, foot, or footprint).

Tewāhi *te* (the); *wāhi* (place). A component of several names.

Te Wai *te* (the); *wai* (water, or stream). A common component of place names, usually followed by a personal name, or name of a plant or tree.

Te Waipounamu The water of greenstone. The Māori name for the South Island. The original form may have been Te Wāhipounamu, the place of greenstone.

Te Waitere *te* (the); *wai* (water); *tere* (swiftly flowing). The place was named in 1905, partly because of its meaning and partly in memory of the Reverend John Whitely, as it is the Māori pronunciation of his name.

Te Waka-a-Aoraki The canoe of Aoraki; an old name for the South Island. While exploring the southern ocean, Aoraki's canoe was caught in a storm and turned to stone, becoming the South Island.

Te Waka-a-Māui The canoe of Māui, from which the mythical hero fished up the North Island. An old name for the South Island.

Te Weka *te* (the); *weka* (woodhen).

Te Wera *te* (the); *wera* (heat, or burning).

Te Wētā *te* (the); *wētā* (large native insect).

Te Whāiti *te* (the); *whāiti* (narrow gorge). The full name is Te Whāitinui-a-Toi, the great canyon of Toi.

Te Whakaraupō *te* (the); *whaka* (South Island form of *whanga*: harbour); *raupō* (reed). Harbour of the raupō reed, the Māori name for Lyttelton Harbour.

Te Whanganui-a-Tara *te* (the); *whanganui* (great harbour); *a* (of); *Tara* (ancestor of Ngāi Tara). The great harbour of Tara, Wellington Harbour or Port Nicholson. Another theory is that it means The great waiting of Tara, who waited to take revenge on enemies who had killed and eaten his dog.

Te Whata *te* (the); *whata* (food storehouse). Īhenga raised a foodstore here.

Te Whetū *te* (the); *whetū* (star).

Temuka Correctly, Te-umu-kaha; *te* (the); *umu* (oven); *kaha* (strong). The fierce oven. Another meaning given to the name is Strong current, umu here meaning current.

Tēpene Māori form of the name of a missionary, Stephenson.

Tīhaka A kind of basket.

Tīkapa Plaintive, mournful

Tīkapa Moana *tīkapa* (plaintive, mournful); *moana* (ocean). The Māori name for the Hauraki Gulf.

Tikinui *tiki* (carved figure in wood or greenstone); *nui* (big). Large tiki.

Tiki: greenstone image

Tikitapu *tiki* (carved figure); *tapu* (sacred). A young woman lost a greenstone tiki while she was bathing in the lake. The Māori name for the Blue Lake.

Tikitere A contraction of Taku-tiki-i-tere-nei, My youngest daughter who floated away. The young woman jumped into a

boiling pool. Tiki is an endearing contraction of pōtiki, last-born.
Tikitiki   Girdle, or knot of hair.
Tikokino   *tiko* (evacuation of the bowels); *kino* (bad).
Tikorangi   *tiko* (to protrude); *rangi* (sky). Sky piercer.
Tikorauaruhe   The latrine in the bracken fern.
Tīmaru   *tī* (cabbage-tree); *maru* (shelter). The correct name is probably **Te Maru**, the place of shelter.
Tīmatanga   The beginning, or starting point.
Tinaaruhe   *tina* (fixed); *aruhe* (fern-root). To be prevented from eating fern-root.
Tinakori   Correctly, Tinakore. *Tina* (Māori form of the word dinner); *kore* (none). No dinner. Māori workmen on the road forgot to take their dinners with them. The hill (properly Ōtari) may have been named after the road. It is now known as Te Ahumairangi.
Tiniroto   *tini* (many); *roto* (lakes). Many lakes. A modern descriptive name.
Tinopai   *tino* (very); *pai* (good).
Tīnui   *tī* (cabbage-tree); *nui* (many). Many cabbage-trees.
Tioripātea   *tiori* (to hold up to view); *pātea* (clear). The Māori name for the Haast Pass. A leader of the group of travellers called out that the path was clear.
Tīpapa   *tī* (cabbage-tree); *papa* (flat). Cabbage-tree flat.
Tiraora   *tira* (a company of travellers); *ora* (satisfied). The original name of the bay was Tira, but ora was added to distinguish it from Tīrau.
Tiratū   Mast of a canoe.
Tīrau   *tī* (cabbage-tree); *rau* (many). Many cabbage-trees.
Tīraumea   Many waving cabbage-trees.
Tiritiri-matangi   *tiritiri* (a twig that indicates the position of a kūmara tuber); *matangi* (the warm north-east breeze). Originally Tiritiri-o-Matangi, a name

Tī: cabbage-tree

brought from Polynesia, meaning
The sanctified heaven of fragrant
breezes.

Tirohanga   View.

Tirohia   Look, or behold.

Tiroiti   Circumscribed view.

Tiromoana   *tiro* (view); *moana* (ocean). Sea view.

Tironui   *tiro* (view); *nui* (great). Great view.

Tiropahī   *tiro* (view); *pahī* (a large sea-going canoe with sails). View of a large canoe.

Tiroroa   *tiro* (view); *roa* (long). Extensive view.

Tītahi   *tī* (cabbage-tree); *tahi* (single). A single cabbage-tree.

Tītī   Mutton bird.

Titirangi   *titi* (long streaks of cloud); *rangi* (sky). Long streaks of cloud in the sky. Or **Tītīrangi**, a species of veronica. Titirangi in Auckland is popularly translated as Fringe of heaven.

Titiroa   Very long streaks of cloud.

Tititea   *titi* (peak); *tea* (white). Steep peak of glistening white. The Māori name for Mount Aspiring.

Tītoki   A native tree.

Tītri   A corruption of the Pākehā name tea-tree (for mānuka). The name is now Tī Tree Point.

Toa: warrior

Toa   Male, brave, or warrior.

Toatoa   A native tree.

Toetoes   (Bay and Harbour) Named after a Māori chief, Toitoi or Toetoe.

Toka   Rock.

Tokaanu   *toka* (stone); *anu* (cold). A cold stone.

Tokakaroro   *toka* (rock); *karoro* (sea-gull). Sea-gull rock.

Tokanui   *toka* (rock); *nui* (many). Plenty of rocks.

Tokarahi   *toka* (rock); *rahi* (many). Many rocks, because of the many blocks of limestone.

Tokaroa   *toka* (rock); *roa* (long). Long rock. The Māori name for Meola Reef, Auckland, among other locations.

Tokatoka   Rocks upon rocks. A descriptive name for the lava crag above Wairoa.

Tokerau Correctly, Tokarau. *Toka* (rocks); *rau* (hundred, or many). A hundred rocks. The Māori name for the Bay of Islands.

Tokirima *toki* (adze); *rima* (five). Five adzes.

Toko Pole, or to propel.

Tokoiti *toko* (pole); *iti* (small). Little poles. Or possibly, Tokaiti, little rocks. Also means few people.

Tokomaru The canoe on which Manaia came to Aotearoa/New Zealand. Literally, *toko* (staff); *maru* (shade or shelter).

Tokoroa *toko* (pole); *roa* (long). Long pole.

Tokotea Correctly, Tokatea. *Toka* (stone); *tea* (white). White rock. Kahumatamomoe placed a white rock on a hill in memory of his father, Tamatekapua.

Tolaga An obvious corruption of a Māori name. One conjecture is that when Captain Cook recorded the name he pointed north-west to the mainland and asked what the place was called. The Māori may have thought he was asking the name of the wind, and replied Tarakaka, south-west wind. The original name of Tolaga Bay was Uawā, q.v.

Tōmoana Named after a chief. Literally, *tō* (to drag); *moana* (ocean).

Tongapōrutu *tonga* (south wind); *pō* (night); *rutu* (to drive into). Driving into a southerly at night. Whātonga's canoe Kurahaupō was running down the west coast when it struck a southerly here at nightfall.

Tongariro *tonga* (south wind); *riro* (carried away). When Ngātoroirangi was on the summit and in danger of perishing from the cold, he called to his sisters in Hawaiki for fire. His words were carried on the wings of the south wind. This name was originally applied to the three peaks, Tongariro, Ngāuruhoe and Ruapehu.

Tōpuni Close together, or a black dogskin cloak.

Tōrea Oyster-catcher.

Tōrere Named after a woman who swam ashore from the Tainui canoe. Literally, to hurry, or fall headlong.

Tōtara A native tree. Tōtara in North Otago was so named because it was the only one of its kind in that district. At one time this place was called Tōtaratahi, a single tōtara.

Tōtaranui

Tōtaranui *tōtara* (tree); *nui* (many). Many totara.

Tōwai A native tree.

Tuahiwi *tua* (on the other side); *hiwi* (ridge). On the other side of the ridge.

Tuai Dark.

Tūākau *tū* (to stand); *ākau* (shore or coast). To stand by the shore of the river. There was a commanding view down the Waikato River for some miles from this place.

Tuamarina Correctly, Tuamarino. *Tua* (beyond); *marino* (calm). Clear view from the plains to the hills.

Tuapeka *tua* (beyond); *peka* (branch of a river). On the further side of the stream.

Tuatapere A sacred ceremony before a time for amusement. There has been a suggestion that the name should be Tuatapera, pout of the lips from water being bitter.

Tuatara A native reptile.

Tūhawaiki Named after a famous Māori chief of Otago, known by early settlers as Bloody Jack.

Tūhua Obsidian. Also the Māori name for Mayor Island, named by Toi. It is an extinct volcano and there are large deposits of obsidian.

Tūrangārere

Tūī Native bird.

Tukituki To demolish, or batter. See Ruatāhuna.

Tumahu Healed (of a wound).

Tūmai *tū* (to stand); *mai* (this way, or towards the person speaking).

Tūmoana *tū* (to stand); *moana* (ocean, or lake). Standing in the lake.

Tuna Eel.

Tunanui *tuna* (eel); *nui* (many). Plenty of eels.

Tuparoa *tupa* (shellfish); *roa* (long). Long shellfish.

Turakina To be felled or thrown down. Hau, when pursuing his wife, named the stream because a tree was lying across it.

Tūranga *tūranga* (standing).

Tūranga-a-Kupe *tūranga* (wounding, resting); *a* (of); *Kupe*. Kupe stayed here and may have injured himself. The place is now Seatoun in Wellington.

Tūranga-nui-a-Kiwa The great standing of Kiwa. It was a stopping place of Toi's canoe, and was on the site of modern Gisborne. Kiwa waited for days here for the arrival of his son Kahutuanui.

Tūrangārere Correctly, Tūranga-a-rere. *Tūranga*

(standing); *a* (of); *rere* (to fly or wave). It was a place where a taua (war party) stood with feathers waving in their hair.

Tūrangawaewae *tūranga* (standing); *waewae* (feet). A standing place for the feet; this is a multi-layered concept in Māori culture that refers to the place a person can call home.

Tūrangi Named after a chief. Literally, *tū* (to stand); *rangi* (sky). To stand in the sky.

Tūrehu Fairies.

Turiroa *turi* (post); *roa* (long). Long post.

Turua Beautiful, referring to the reflections in the river.

Turuturumōkai *turuturu* (to set a post in the ground); *mōkai* (slave). A slave was captured on the spot where the post was set in.

Tūtaekurī *tūtae* (dung); *kurī* (dog).

Tūtaenui *tūtae* (dung); *nui* (big). The Māori name for Marton.

Tūtāmoe *tū* (to rise up); *tāmoe* (flat top). Mountain rising up with a flat top.

Tūtira Row, or file.

Tūtoko Named after a chief. Literally, *tū* (to stand); *toko* (post). To stand up like a post.

Tutukākā *tutu* (a tree in which snares are set); *kākā* (parrot). The kākā perch.

Tuturau *tutu* (native tree); *rau* (many). Many tutu trees.

Tututawa *tutu* (to steep in water); *tawa* (a native tree). The place where the tawa berries are steeped in water.

Uawā *ua* (rain); *wā* (season). Rainy season. The original name for Tolaga Bay, q.v. Possibly **Ūawa**, to reach land at the river.

Uia To be disentangled.

Umere To keep in time by chanting.

Umukurī *umu* (oven); *kurī* (dog). Dog cooked in the oven. What was cooked in the oven was really Kurīmanga, a tohunga (priest or skilled person).

Umutaoroa *umu* (oven); *tao* (to cook); *roa* (long). The ovens that took a long time to cook. Refers to an incident in a battle between

Ngāti Māmoe and Rangitāne tribes. The site of present-day Dannevirke.

Umutōī *umu* (oven); *tōī* (to be moist).

Umuwheke *umu* (oven); *wheke* (octopus). Octopus cooked in an oven.

Upokongaro *upoko* (head); *ngaro* (hidden). Hidden head. Irangārangi was disconsolate when her brothers were killed and she died of grief. Lest she be mutilated by enemies, her people cut off her head and hid it in a cave by this stream.

Upokopōito *upoko* (head); *pōito* (float). Heads like floats on a fishing net. Some Māori were drowned here, and their heads bobbed up and down like floats on the water. This was near the foreshore at Napier.

Upokororo A freshwater fish.

Urenui Manaia named the river after his son Tū-urenui. Literally, *ure* (figurative expression for courage); *nui* (big). Great courage.

Urewera *ure* (penis); *wera* (burnt). The name was given almost sarcastically because a chief received a severe burn when he rolled into a fire while asleep.

Urupukapuka *uru* (grove); *pukapuka* (shrub). A grove of pukapuka.

Urutī *uru* (grove); *tī* (cabbage-tree). A grove of cabbage-trees.

Uruwhenua *uru* (west); *whenua* (land). West country.

Utiku A Biblical name, Eutychus, in its Māori form. The name was chosen by the chief Pōtaka when he came under missionary influence.

W

Waenga In the middle.

Waerenga A clearing.

Waerenga-a-Hika *waerenga* (a clearing); *a* (of); *Hika* (a chief). Hika's clearing.

Waerenga-o-Kurī *waerenga* (a clearing); *o* (of); *Kurī* (name of a chief). Kurī's clearing.

Waharoa Named after the great chief Te Waharoa. Literally *waha* (mouth); *roa* (long), i.e., the gateway to a palisaded village.

Waianakārua *wai* (water); *ana*

Waharoa: entrance to pā

(cave); *kā* (Southern form of *ngā*, the); *rua* (two). Water from two caves, or the meeting of waters. Or else the creek of Nakarua.

Waiāniwa Probably a contraction of Waiāniwaniwa, q.v.

Waiāniwaniwa *wai* (water); *āniwaniwa* (rainbow, or deep). Deep water, or water where rainbows appear in the spray.

Waiapu *wai* (water); *apu* (to swallow). Swallowing waters. The river is dangerous to cross in time of flood. Or it might be a reference to a special kind of stone found only in this district, used for polishing adzes.

Waiareka *wai* (water); *a* (of); *reka* (sweetness). Sweet or pleasant water. Also a name for the Rotorua/Bay of Plenty region.

Waiari *wai* (water); *ari* (clear). Clear water.

Waiariki Hot springs, or curative waters. They are the ariki, chiefs or patriarchs of all water. Also a name for the Rotorua/Bay of Plenty region.

Waiaruhe *wai* (water); *aruhe* (edible fern-root). Stream where the fern-root can be obtained.

Waiatarua *waiata* (song); *rua* (two). Two songs. Or *wai* (water); *atarua* (two images). Double-imaged water. The Māori name for Lake St John, Auckland, now drained.

Waiatarua in the Waitakere Ranges took its name from a guesthouse in the area.

Waiau *wai* (water); *au* (current). River of swirling currents.

Waiaua *wai* (water); *aua* (native fish). Kahumatamomoe and Huarere saw the fish in the river and conferred the name.

Waiautoa See Waiauuha.

Waiauuha *wai* (water); *au* (current); *uha* (female). The female Waiau. The male river was Waiautoa (Clarence River). Their sources are close together. In legend they were lovers who drifted apart, and weep for each other.

Waiawa *wai* (water); *awa* (valley). River in the valley.

Waihāhā *wai* (water); *hāhā* (noisy). Noisy water.

Waihao *wai* (water); *hao* (a small eel). Eel river. The name is common. The South Canterbury river was named and discovered by a chief whose wife found these eels particularly acceptable.

Waihapa *wai* (water); *hapa* (crooked). Crooked stream.

Waiharakeke *wai* (water); *harakeke* (flax). Water where the flax grows. At Blenheim the Māori name has been changed to the English equivalent, Flaxbourne.

Waiharara A corruption of Waiharere or Waihārearea. *Wai* (water); *hārearea* (heard indistinctly).

Waiharuru *wai* (water); *haruru* (resounding). Rumbling or resounding water, descriptive of the Whakarewarewa area.

Waihau *wai* (water); *hau* (wind). Windy water.

Waiheke *wai* (water); *heke* (to ebb or drip). Ebbing water.

Waihemo *wai* (water); *hemo* (to disappear). Disappearing water, referring to the river when the tide has gone out.

Waihī *wai* (water); *hī* (gushing forth). Water gushing out. An old name from Hawaiki.

Waihihī Gushing water, a name from Hawaiki.

Waihīnau *wai* (water); *hīnau* (native tree). Hīnau trees by the water.

Waihīrere *wai* (water); *hīrere* (to rush). Rushing waters.

Waiho Correctly, Waiau.

Waihōaka *wai* (water); *hōaka* (South Island form of *hōanga*: sandstone). Sandstone stream.

Waihola *wai* (water); *hola* (a rendering of *hora*: spread out). Spreading waters. It is a wide, shallow lake.

Waihopai *waiho* (leave); *pai* (well). It may be a corruption of Wai-o-pai, The water of Pai. The Māori name for Invercargill.

Waihopo *wai* (water); *hopo* (to be apprehensive). River that one fears to cross.

Waihora *wai* (water); *hora* (spread out). Wide expanse of water. Lake Ellesmere.

Waihou *wai* (water); *hou* (cold, or new). New or cold river. Probably New river, in the sense that it has cut a new channel.

Waihua *wai* (water); *hua* (fish roe). So named by a Māori man because his dog ate a porcupine fish there, but left the roe.

Waiiti *wai* (water); *iti* (little). Little river.

Waikaia Correctly, Waikea or Waikeha. *Wai* (water); *keha* (bur). The stream where the keha grew. Rākaihautū named it because the native bur infested the place.

Waikākahi Shortened to **Waikaka** in the Southland locality, near Gore. *Wai* (water); *kākahi* (shellfish). Water where the shellfish may be found.

Waikākaho *wai* (water); *kākaho* (plumes of the toetoe). Toetoe-plume water.

Waikana Short for Waikanakana. *Wai* (water); *kanakana* (lamprey). Lamprey river.

Waikanae *wai* (water); *kanae* (mullet). Hau, who was searching for his wife, looked about out of the corner of his eye (ka ngahae ngā pī), and likened his eyes to the glistening of the mullet.

Waikaraka *wai* (water); *karaka* (native tree). Karaka river.

Waikare *wai* (water); *kare* (to ripple). Rippling water.

Waikareiti *wai* (water); *kare* (to ripple); *iti* (little). See Waikaremoana.

Waikaremoana *wai* (water); *kare* (to ripple); *moana* (lake). Popularly rendered The sea of rippling waters, but it would be better as The sea of dashing waters, because the waves were agitated by the taniwha who formed the Waikaretāheke, the raging torrent that runs out of the lake.

Waikāretu *wai* (water); *kāretu* (sweet-scented grass). Kāretu river.

Waikari Ditch or trench. Waikari in Hawke's Bay commemorates Paoa's dog Whākao, who dug (*kari* means to dig) until he found water (*wai*).

Waikato *wai* (water); *kato* (to flow). Full flowing river.

Waikaukau *wai* (water); *kaukau* (to bathe). Bathing place.

Waikāura *wai* (water); *kāura* (a form of *kōura*: crayfish). Crayfish were plentiful in this stream.

Waikawa *wai* (water); *kawa* (bitter). Bitter water.

Waikawau *wai* (water); *kawau* (shag). Shag river.

Waikererū *wai* (water); *kererū* (wood pigeon). Kererū water.

Waikeria *wai* (water); *keria* (dug out). A gouged-out watercourse.

Waikerikeri *wai* (water); *kerikeri* (rushing along violently). The

Māori name for the Selwyn River.

Waikēwai Correctly, Waikēkēwai; *wai* (water); *kēkēwai* (small dragonfly). Dragonfly stream.

Waikiekie *wai* (water); *kiekie* (climbing plant). Kiekie water.

Waikimihia *wai* (water); *kimihia* (sought for). The sought-for water, the Māori name for Hinemoa's Bath on Mokoia Island, to which Hinemoa swam from the mainland and in which she bathed on her arrival.

Waikino *wai* (water); *kino* (bad). Unpleasant water.

Waikite *wai* (water); *kite* (to see). The once-famous geyser at Whakarewarewa could be seen clearly from Rotorua.

Waikiwi *wai* (water); *kiwi* (flightless bird). Kiwi stream.

Waikōau *wai* (water); *kōau* (shag). Shag river.

Waikohu Mist or fog.

Waikoikoi *wai* (water); *koikoi* (cool). Cool water.

Waikōkopu *wai* (water); *kōkopu* (freshwater fish). Kōkopu stream.

Waikōkōwai *wai* (water); *kōkōwai* (red ochre). Water where red ochre is found.

Waikomiti *wai* (water); *komiti* (mingled). Mingled waters. The Māori name for Glen Eden.

Waikōpua *wai* (water); *kōpua* (deep). Deep water.

Waikorohihī Bubbling or hissing water, a pool at Whakarewarewa.

Waikotūturi *wai* (water); *kotūturi* (kneeling). The water of kneeling. Some defeated warriors were forced to kneel beside the stream with their hands tied behind their backs.

Waikouaiti *wai* (water); *koua*, or *kua* (to become); *iti* (small). The water that decreased. The usual explanation of this name is that the river changed its course, the flow thus decreasing at this point.

Waikōura *wai* (water); *kōura* (crayfish). Crayfish stream.

Waikōwhai *wai* (water); *kōwhai* (flowering tree). Many kōwhai grew here.

Waikumete *wai* (water); *kumete* (wooden bowl). Kumete creek.

Kumete: wooden bowl

Waikuta *wai* (water); *kuta* (a rush). Stream of rushes. The name was given by Īhenga because of the profuse growth of rushes.

Waimā *wai* (water); *mā* (white). White river. There was a great deal of white limestone in its bed.

Waimaero *wai* (water); *maero* (wild man of the forest). The name is also said to mean deep water channel, or hard water.

Waimāhaka *wai* (water); *māhaka* (South Island form of *māhanga*: twin). Twin waters.

Waimahora *wai* (water); *mahora* (to spread out). Spreading waters.

Waimahuru *wai* (water); *mahuru* (placid). Placid waters. The name was given by Paoa because of the appearance of the stream.

Waimai Probably the original name was Waimataī. *Wai* (water); *mataī* (black pine). Black pine river.

Waimakariri *wai* (water); *makariri* (cold). Cold river.

Waimamaku *wai* (water); *mamaku* (tree-fern). Mamaku stream.

Waimana *wai* (water); *mana* (shrimp). Stream in which shrimps are caught.

Waimanarara *wai* (water); *manarara* (noisy). Turbulent river.

Waimangaroa *wai* (water); *manga* (branch); *roa* (long). Long branch of a river.

Waimangeo *wai* (water); *mangeo* (pungent, mineralised water). The Māori name for Alum Creek.

Waimangu *wai* (water); *mangu* (black). Black water. The name of the famous extinct geyser that threw a huge volume of muddy water high into the air.

Waimanu *wai* (water); *manu* (bird). Stream frequented by birds.

Waimarama *wai* (water); *marama* (moonlight). Moonlit water.

Waimārama Clear water.

Waimarie *wai* (water); *marie* (quiet). Quiet waters. Waimarie also means fortunate.

Waimarino *wai* (water); *marino* (calm, or still). Still waters.

Waimaru *wai* (water); *maru* (sheltered). Calm water.

Waimatā *wai* (water); *matā* (bullet). Stream where bullets are found. A running fight took place there in the nineteenth century, and it is said that bullets were afterwards to be found in the bed of the stream.

Waimātaitai *wai* (water); *mātaitai* (salty). Brackish water. A descriptive name for a lagoon.

Waimate *wai* (water); *mate* (stagnant). The original name in the South Island was Waimatemate, with the same meaning. Until floods came, the creeks became blocked up and there were many stagnant pools.

Waimatenui *wai* (water); *mate* (stagnant); *nui* (big). Great expanse of stagnant water.

Waimatuku *wai* (water); *matuku* (bittern). Bittern stream.

Waimauku *wai* (water); *mauku* (small fern). A river that when flooded drowned the cabbage-trees, so that their tops appeared above the water like small ferns.

Waimaunga *wai* (water); *maunga* (mountain). Mountain stream.

Waimea Several meanings have been given for the name. *Wai* (water); *mea* (unimportant, forgotten). The stream with the forgotten name. Mea may be a contraction of meha (tasteless). The use of the name is widespread, and could mean insipid, tasteless, unimportant, lonely, unpalatable, etc.

Waimeha See Waimea.

Waimiha Probably another form of Waimea, q.v. It may mean Water that is pretty to look at.

Waimihi *wai* (water); *mihi* (to sigh, regret or greet).

Waimiro *wai* (water); *miro* (native tree). Miro creek.

Waimoari *wai* (water); *moari* (giant swing). The river beside which a moari was erected.

Moari: giant swing

Waimori *wai* (water); *mori* (without tributaries).

Waimotu *wai* (water); *motu* (island). Island stream, or stream with an island in it.

Wainamu *wai* (water); *namu* (sandfly). Stream infested with sandflies.

Wainihinihi *wai* (water); *nihinihi* (to glide past). The place where the waters glide past.

Wainono *wai* (water); *nono* (oozing). Oozing water.

Wainui *wai* (water); *nui* (big). Big river, bay or expanse of water.

Wainuiomata *wai* (water); *nui* (big); *o* (of); *Mata* (person's name). Big stream belonging to Mata.

Waingaro *wai* (water); *ngaro* (lost). Hidden waters.

Waingawa Correctly, Waiawanga, water of hesitation. Hau hesitated to cross this river when in pursuit of his wife.

Waingongoro *wai* (water); *ngongoro* (gurgling), it also means snoring, and this is the place where Turi snored.

Waioeka Probably Waioweka. *Wai* (water); *o* (of); *weka* (woodhen). Weka river.

Waiomatatini The syllables are capable of so many meaningless translations that speculation is idle. It is the place where an ancestor of the Ngāti Porou tribe was hung up in a pūriri tree, the incident being remembered by the giving of the famous name Tūwhakairiora.

Waiomū *wai* (water); *o* (of); *Mū* (personal name). The water of Mū.

Waione *wai* (water); *one* (beach). Stream on the beach.

Waiongona *wai* (water); *o* (of); *Ngona* (personal name). Water of Ngona.

Waiopani *wai* (water); *o* (of); *pani* (orphan). Orphan water or lake.

Waiora-a-Tāne *wai* (water); *ora* (living); *a* (of); *Tāne* (the god of nature). A very famous name in mythology.

Waiorongomai *wai* (water); *o* (of); *Rongomai* (personal name). The water of Rongomai.

Waiotapu Sacred waters.

Waiotemarama *wai* (water); *o* (of); *te* (the); *marama* (moon). The waters of the moon. A legend tells of the moon coming down to drink the water here.

Waiotira *wai* (water); *o* (of); *tira* (sticks set up for purposes of divination). Water of incantation.

Waiotū *wai* (water); *o* (of); *Tū* (the god of war). A pool or stream where ceremonies were rendered to Tū (or in full, Tūmatauenga).

Waiouru *wai* (water); *o* (of); *uru* (west). River of the west. The stream is the most westerly branch of the Hautupu River.

Waipā *wai* (water); *pā* (fortified village). River by the pā.

Waipahī *wai* (water); *pahī* (flowing). Flowing water, or The water of Pahi, a chief who was born alongside the river.

Waipango *wai* (water); *pango* (black). Black water.

Waipao *wai* (water); *pao* (to strike). The place was named after Waipao, who was killed by Tūwhakairiora.

Waipaoa *wai* (water); *paoa* (smoky). Smoky water. In fact it should be called Wai-o-Paoa, the river of Paoa, a famous chief whose people had made a canoe in the forest. He created the river to launch the canoe.

Waipapa *wai* (water); *papa* (flat, or flat rock). Stream across the plain, or stream of the flat rock.

Waipapakauri *wai* (water); *papa* (flat land); *kauri* (native tree). Swampy ground where the kauri grows.

Waipara *wai* (water); *para* (mud). River with a thick muddy sediment.

Waipata *wai* (water); *pata* (dripping). Dripping water.

Waipātiki *wai* (water); *pātiki* (flounder). Water where the flounders may be found.

Waipatukahu *wai* (water); *patu* (to beat); *kahu* (cloak). Water in which garments were beaten.

Waipawa *wai* (water); *pawa* (bird-snare). Waipawa in Hawke's Bay is named after Pawa or Paoa, but has also been rendered Waipawamate, water smelling strongly, or dead water.

Waipīata *wai* (water); *pīata* (glistening). Glistening water.

Waipipi *wai* (water); *pipi* (shellfish). Where the pipi are found.

Waipiro *wai* (water); *piro* (stinking). Evil-smelling water.

Waipori Correctly, Waipōuri. *Wai* (water); *pōuri* (dark). Dark river.

Waipoua *wai* (water); *poua* (shellfish). The original name was probably Waipoa, poa being a shellfish found at the mouth of the river. Another conjecture is that the name is **Waipōua**: *wai* (water); *pō* (night); *ua* (rain); water that comes from the rain at night.

Waipounamu *wai* (water); *pounamu* (greenstone). Greenstone river. See Te Waipounamu.

Waipōuri *wai* (water); *pōuri* (dark). Dark stream.

Waipū *wai* (water); *pū* (red). Reddish water. A fairly persistent belief is that *pū* refers to the sound of gunfire.

Waipuku *wai* (water); *puku* (to swell). Swelling water.

Waipukurau *wai* (water); *pukurau* (a large white mushroom). Stream where the mushrooms grow. This is the correct meaning, but it has been conjectured that the name should have been Waipukerau. *Waipuke* (flood); *rau* (many). Many floods.

Wairākei *wai* (water); *rākei* (adorning). The place where the pools were used as mirrors.

Wairaki *wai* (water); *raki* (dry). Dried-up waters. It is the bed of an old lake.

Wairangi Foolish, or excited.

Wairarapa *wai* (water); *rarapa* (glistening). Glistening waters. When Hau saw the beautiful lake and valley his eyes glistened with delight. The glistening is not only of the water but of his eyes.

Wairau *wai* (water); *rau* (many). The plain of a hundred rivers. Simple names often have many meanings, and some that have been given for Wairau are, The rift in the clouds, Waters of many streams, and Discoloured waters. The Māori name for Blenheim.

Waireka *wai* (water); *reka* (sweet). Pleasant waters.

Wairepo *wai* (water); *repo* (swamp). Swampy water, or Water running through a swamp.

Wairere Waterfall.

Wairewa *wai* (water); *rewa* (to lift up). Water lifted up. It is the Māori name for Lake Forsyth, the last lake Rākaihautū scooped out. As the sign that his labours were over, he thrust his kō (digging stick) into the summit of a hill close by named Tuhiraki, and this was the 'lifting up'.

Wairima *wai* (water); *rima* (five).

Wairio *wai* (water); *rio* (dried up). Dried-up waters. Another conjecture is that the name should be Waireo. *Wai* (water); *reo* (voice). Voice of the waters.

Wairoa *wai* (water); *roa* (long). Usually Long river, but in some places it means High waterfall, and in one case Tall geyser.

Wairongoā *wai* (water); *rongoā* (medicine). Water with curative properties.

Wairongomai Probably the correct form is Wai-o-Rongomai, the water of Rongomai.

Wairua Soul or spirit. Or *wai* (water); *rua* (two). Two streams.

Wairuna *wai* (water); *runa* (dock plant). Stream where the dock grows.

Wairunga *wai* (water); *runga* (above, or from above). Stream that flows from the mountains.

Waitaha *wai* (water); *taha* (to pass on one side). Backwater. Some South Island names come from the Waitaha tribe. Also a name for the Canterbury Plains, an abbreviation of Kā-pākihi-whakateketeka-a-Waitaha, q.v.

Waitahanui *wai* (water); *tahanui* (a variety of cabbage-tree). Stream where the cabbage trees grow. Or Big backwater.

Waitahora *wai* (water); *tahora* (spread out, or a small duck). Duck stream, or Spreading waters.

Waitāhuna *wai* (water); *tāhuna* (sandbank). Usually translated as Stream of many sandbanks, it was actually named after a Ngāi Tahu chief.

Waitai *wai* (water); *tai* (tide). Tidal or brackish water.

Waitākaro *wai* (water); *tākaro* (to play or wrestle). Stream running through a games area.

Waitakaruru *wai* (water); *takaruru* (stagnant). Stagnant water. One amusing meaning has been given: *wai* (water); *taka* (to fall); *ruru* (owl). Water that the morepork fell into.

Waitakere *wai* (water); *takere* (deep). Deep pools. Another meaning is Cascading waters. The Auckland Waitakere takes its name from a large rock at the mouth of the Waitakere River, which the waves would sweep over. The South Island Waitakere (Nile River) was originally Ngāwaitakerei, The waters of Takerei.

Waitaki *wai* (water); *taki* (South Island form of *tangi*: sounding). Rumbling waters, coming from the sound of the river over the shingle beds. There is a legend that the river was formed by the tears of two brothers, whose sister was drowned at the mouth of the river and turned into a rock. The brothers were transformed into two hills near Ōhau, and their tears form the river of weeping.

Waitangi *wai* (water); *tangi* (weeping, or sounding). Noisy or weeping waters.

Waitapu *wai* (water); *tapu* (sacred). Sacred water.

Waitara *wai* (water); *tara* (short for *taranga*: wide steps). River crossed with big steps. Turi forded it with great strides. Another explanation is that it simply means Mountain stream: *tara* (peak); and another that a young man searched for his father by successive throwings of his dart: *whai* (to follow); *tara* (dart).

Waitara on the Mōhaka River is so named because a chief took with him the bones of his slave to scrape and shape into spears (tara).

Waitārere   *wai* (water); *tārere* (to flow copiously). Running streams.

Waitāria   *wai* (water); *tāria* (to wait for). Water that has been waited for.

Waitata   *wai* (water); *tata* (close). Nearby water.

Waitati   The correct name is Waitētē. *Wai* (water); *tētē* (blue duck). Water frequented by blue ducks.

Waitematā   *wai* (water); *te* (the); *matā* (short for *matātūhua*: obsidian). Water as smooth as the surface of obsidian. It may be a coincidence that the name of the upper reaches of the harbour was Waitīmata, *tīmata* (to begin), being a rock that was a tribal boundary.

Waitematamata   *wai* (water); *te* (the); *Matamata* (a taniwha who lived in the creek).

Waitepeka   *wai* (water); *te* (the); *peka* (branch). Tributary of the river.

Waitētē   *wai* (water); *tētē* (dripping). Water dripping from the ground.

Waitetī   *wai* (water); *te* (the); *tī* (cabbage-tree). Cabbage-tree stream.

Waitetuna   *wai* (water); *te* (the); *tuna* (eel). Creek where the eels are caught.

Waitoa   *wai* (water); *toa* (rough). Rough water.

Waitoetoe   *wai* (water); *toetoe* (plume grass). Toetoe stream.

Waitohi   *wai* (water); *tohi* (baptismal rite). Stream where the baptismal rite was performed. In addition to this explanation, there are two others for this, the original name for Picton. It may be, in full, Te Wera-o-Waitohi, the burning of Waitohi. Waitohi, the sister of Te Rauparaha, is reputed to have been burnt to death in a scrub fire. Or it could mean the clearing burnt by Waitohi to make a plantation.

Waitohu   *wai* (water); *tohu* (to point out). Water that showed the way to two fugitives who escaped to the hills.

Waitomo   *wai* (water); *tomo* (shaft). Water entering the cave by means of long shafts.

Waitōtara   *wai* (water); *tōtara* (native tree). River where the tōtara trees were plentiful.

Waitoto   *wai* (water); *toto* (blood). Probably the scene of a battle.

Waitūī   *wai* (water); *tūī* (native bird). Tūī bay or river.

Tōtara: New Zealand tree

Waituna *wai* (water); *tuna* (eel). Eel stream. It is possible that Waituna West received its Māori name because of an orator who lived there. Some eels remain small and immature, and a Māori ideal of oratory was a flow of words of even length.

Waiuku *wai* (water); *uku* (white clay). A high-born woman came here to choose a husband. The first chief presented was good-looking, but did not impress the woman. His brother who was in the kūmara plantation was hurriedly summoned, and scrubbed with white clay from the stream to make him presentable. The uku was known as Māori soap. The story has a happy ending, and the event is commemorated in the name Waiuku.

Waiuta *wai* (water); *uta* (inland). Inland water. Or to load a canoe on the river.

Waiwera *wai* (water); *wera* (hot). Hot water. The Auckland Waiwera is the site of hot springs. The southern Waiwera is named after Waiwhero, a chief.

Waiwhero *wai* (water); *whero* (red). Red water.

Waiwhetū *wai* (water); *whetū* (star). Star-reflecting water.

Waiwhio *wai* (water); *whio* (blue mountain duck, or whistling duck). Stream of the mountain duck.

Whio: blue duck

Wakamarino *waka* (South Island form of *whanga*: harbour); *marino* (peaceful). A peaceful bay.

Wakanui *waka* (canoe); *nui* (big). Large canoe.

Wakapatu Correctly, Whakapatu, to strike, or to kill.

Wakapuaka Correctly, Whakapuaka, the name of Kupe's fishing ground in Tahiti, transferred to Nelson. Literally, *waka* (canoe); *puaka* (dry twigs). The early settlers called it Hokepoke.

Wakarara *waka* (canoe); *rara* (to be thrown broadside on). A canoe thrown on its beam ends.

Wakāri Correctly, Whakaari, to show, or expose to view.

Wakatahuri *waka* (canoe); *tahuri* (overturned). The overturned canoe.

Wakatipu Short for Waka-tipua-waimāori. *Waka* (canoe); *tipua* (enchanted being); *waimāori* (fresh water), Trough of fresh water where the giant lies. The lake was the trough in which the tipua rests, his breathing causing the rise and fall of the lake waters. The original form may be Whakatipu, however; this means to create or cause to grow, so named because the remnants of defeated tribes retired here to rear their families and build up their strength.

Wakatipu-waimāori means Fresh water Wakatipu, and Lake McKerrow is Wakatipu-waitai, Saltwater Wakatipu.

Wakatū *waka* (canoe); *tū* (to pile up). The place where broken canoes were dumped. It is the old name for Nelson; an alternative is Whakatū, *whaka* (to make); *tū* (to stand).

Wānaka This is likely to be the South Island form of *wānanga*, sacred knowledge, or place of learning. Wānanga is the modern term for a university. Another explanation is that it is Ōanaka (which has much the same sound): *ō* (the place of); *Anaka* (name of a person).

Wangaehu See Whangaehu.

Wanganui See Whanganui.

Wangapeka *wanga* (properly *whanga*: harbour or valley); *peka* (edible fern-root). Valley of the fern-root.

Waotū In full, He Wao-tūtahi-ngā-rākau, the place of high trees standing by themselves.

Warea To be absorbed, or to be made unconscious. Possibly named after the wife of Manaia.

Warepā Correctly, Wharepā, fortified house.

Waro A deep pit, or a recess in the rocks.

Weka Wood-hen.

Wekakura *weka* (wood-hen); *kura* (red). Reddish-coloured weka.

Weraroa *wera* (burnt); *roa* (long). Long burn, in preparation for a clearing.

Wingatui Possibly the correct name is Whiringatua, the place of the plaiting of straps. There is a story that comes from the founding of Otago. It is said that one of the settlers shot at and winged a tūī.

Wiri Shortened form of the surname of the chief Takaanini Wirihana. Wirihana is the Māori transliteration for Wilson. Literally, To shiver, or tremble.

WH

Whāingaroa *whāinga* (pursuit); *roa* (long). The Māori name for Raglan Harbour. The Tainui canoe had a long voyage along this coast. It has also been rendered as *whai* (stingray); *ngā* (the); *roa* (long); or *whainga* (possessed); *roa* (long).

Whakaangiangi To make thin.

Whakaari To make visible. The Māori name for White Island, among other places.

Whakahoro To scatter, or to take to pieces.

Whakairi To hang up.

Whakakī To fill. This referred to the lagoon that the Māori liked to see at a high level for fishing and eeling.

Whakakitenga A place where an extensive view can be obtained.

Whakamahi Correctly Whakamahia, Made to work. Some men in Hawke's Bay were forced to work in the cultivations and were fed with human flesh.

Whakamārama To illuminate, or to explain.

Whakamarino To make peaceful.

Whakapara To make a clearing in the forest.

Whakapoungākau *whakapou* (to establish firmly); *ngākau* (heart). The hills of heart's desire. Tānewhakarara went to hunt in these hills and did not return. His sisters Kuiwai and Haungaroa named the range because of the longing their brother had for them and they for him. Before they returned to Hawaiki they made

Whakarewa

hot springs at Tikitere so that their brother could bathe there if he returned.

Whakarewa To cause something to float.

Whakarewarewa The full name is Te Whakarewarewatanga-o-te-ope-a-Wāhiao, the uprising of the war party of Wāhiao. A war party assembled at the geyser area and performed a war dance before going into action.

Whakarongo To listen, or to inform.

Whakataki To go in search of, or to begin a speech.

Whakatāne To act as a man. Wairaka, the daughter of the chief Toroa, jumped ashore from the Mataatua canoe when it was in difficulties, and took a line ashore. Her famous saying on this occasion was, 'Me whakatāne au i au' (I shall act like a man). There are several variations of the story.

Whakatete Disputed ground. A recent name applied to the sacred places where gold prospectors in the Coromandel Peninsula were not permitted to dig.

Whakatiti A leaf used to let the spirit of a dying man escape.

Whakatū *whaka* (to make); *tū* (to stand). To stand up, or to make a

Whangamatā

Whakatū: to make a speech

speech. The modern Māori name for Nelson.

Whakatutu To place an object so that water falls on to it, to hold open a basket, or to fasten a net to a hoop.

Whananaki *whana* (to rush); *naki* (steadily). A steady rush (of water).

Whanawhana To bend backwards and forwards.

Whangaehu *whanga* (harbour); *ehu* (turbid). Ehu also means to bail out, and it is said that when Hau crossed this river, he had to bail out his canoe; or else that he splashed the water with the flat of his taiaha.

Whangakōkō *whanga* (harbour); *kōkō* (a name for the tūī). Tūī harbour.

Whangamatā *whanga* (harbour); *matā* (obsidian). Obsidian is washed ashore here from Mayor Island.

Whangamoa *whanga* (harbour); *moa* (extinct giant bird). Moa haven.

Whangamōmona *whanga* (valley); *mōmona* (fat). Fertile valley. There is also a story that a man named Hoti waylaid travellers and killed and ate the plump ones.

Whanganui *whanga* (harbour); *nui* (big). Great harbour. Because Māori pronunciation in the Whanganui region substitutes w for wh, the name was recorded as Wanganui and this became the accepted spelling. Either Whanganui or Wanganui are now used officially for the city, and the river takes the form Whanganui.

Whanganui-o-Hei The great bay of Hei. The Māori name for Mercury Harbour.

Whangapara *whanga* (harbour); *para* (sediment). Muddy harbour.

Whangaparāoa *whanga* (harbour); *parāoa* (sperm whale). Whale harbour. This is a place where voyaging canoes landed. A whale was stranded on the beach and became an object of dispute between the men of the Tainui and Arawa canoes.

Whangapē It is said that the name means Waiting for the inside of the pāua. The name comes from the Society Islands.

Whangapipiro Evil-smelling place. This was the hot spring in which the bird-ogress who chased Hatupatu was killed.

Whangapoua *whanga* (harbour); *poua* (shellfish). Harbour of shellfish.

Whāngārā In full Whāngārā-mai-tawhiti. *Whanga* (harbour); *rā* (sun); *mai* (from); *tawhiti* (Tahiti; distant). The name was given by the ancestor Paikea when the bay here reminded him of a place called Whāngārā in his homeland, most likely Tahiti.

Whangarae *whanga* (harbour); *rae* (headland). The bay of many capes, the Māori name for Croisilles Harbour.

Parāoa: sperm whale

Whangarātā *whanga* (harbour); *rātā* (native tree). Bay of rātā trees.

Whāngārei *whanga* (harbour); *rei* (cherished possession). It has been translated as Bountiful harbour. It probably means The waiting of Rei. A young woman Reipae from Waikato waited here for her lover, but grew tired and married another young man. Her sister Reitū married the rejected lover.

But the name has been given many other interpretations, incluing Whāngarei-terenga-parāoa: *whanga* (harbour); *rei* (rushing); *terenga* (place of swimming); *parāoa* (whale).

Whangaroa *whanga* (harbour); *roa* (long).

Whangaruru *whanga* (harbour); *ruru* (sheltered). Sheltered harbour.

Whangateau *whanga* (harbour); *te* (the); *au* (current). The harbour with the strong current.

Whangatoetoe *whanga* (harbour); *toetoe* (plume grass). Toetoe bay.

Whare House. The name is usually given by Pākehā, as in Whare Flat.

Whareātea *whare* (house); *ātea* (space, or out of the way). A large house to accommodate everyone. Such a house stood here for the entertainment of guests long ago.

Wharehine *whare* (house); *hine* (young woman). The house of girls.

Wharehunga *whare* (house); *hunga* (company of people). A large house in which to accommodate people.

Wharehuia *whare* (house); *huia* (extinct bird). Home of the huia.

Wharekauri *whare* (house); *kauri* (native tree). House of the kauri; one of the Māori names for Chatham Island. See Rēkohu.

Wharekōpae House with a door at the side (an unusual place for the door).

Wharekurī Correctly, Te Warokurī, the chasm of the dog.

Wharemā *whare* (house); *mā* (free from tapu). Common house.

Wharemauku *whare* (house); *mauku* (fern). House built of fern-trees.

Wharenui A variety of flax.

Whareorino *whare* (house); *o* (of); *rino* (iron). Corrugated iron house.

Wharepāina *whare* (house); *pāina* (to warm oneself). It has been suggested that as it is in a region of pine plantations, paina stands for pine. The house in the pines.

Wharepapa *whare* (house); *papa* (flat land). House on the flat.

Wharepoa *whare* (house); *poa* (sacred food). House of sacred food.

Whareponga *whare* (house); *ponga* (tree-fern). Tree-fern house.

Wharerākau *whare* (house); *rākau* (timber, or tree). House of timber, or house among the trees.

Wharerātā *whare* (house); *rātā* (native tree). House among the rātā.

Whareroa *whare* (house); *roa* (long). Long house.

Wharetoa *whare* (house); *toa* (warriors). House of men.

Wharetōtara *whare* (house); *tōtara* (native tree). The house made of tōtara bark.

Wharetukura *whare* (house); *tukura* (a species of fern-tree). Fern-tree house.

Whataarama *whata* (food-store); *a* (of); *Rama* (name of a man). The food-store of Rama, the Māori name for the Torlesse Range as well as a peak in the Southern Alps.

Whatamongo Correctly, Whatamangō; *whata* (food-store); *mangō* (shark). Storehouse for shark flesh.

Whataroa *whata* (storehouse); *roa* (long). Long storehouse.

Whatatutu *whata* (storehouse); *tutu* (shrub). Storehouse near the tutu bushes.

Whatawhata Elevated food-store.

Whatitiri Thunder. Īhenga chanted a karakia on the hill, and the thunder roared as the chant ended.

Whātoro To stretch out, or to thrust forward.

Whau A native tree. The Māori name for Avondale, Auckland.

Whāwhāpō *whāwhā* (to feel about); *pō* (night). A young chief crawled into a camp and felt about with his hands at night.

Whāwhārua *whāwhā* (to feel about); *rua* (pit). To feel about in the store pit.

Whekenui *wheke* (octopus); *nui* (big). Te Wheke-a-Muturangi is the name of the huge octopus that Kupe chased across Cook Strait and finally killed in Whekenui Bay.

Whenuahou *whenua* (land); *hou* (new). New country.

Whenuakite The full name, compressed by early Pākehā to Fenukit, is Te Whenua-i-kite-te-manu-aute-o-Tamapahore, the land discovered by the paper-mulberry kite of Tamapahore. This man flew a kite at Remuera. The string broke. The kite was followed until it came to earth at this place.

Whenuakura *whenua* (land); *kura* (red). The name was brought from Hawaiki by Turi of the Aotea canoe, and given in memory of the red feathers of a tropical bird.

Whenuanui *whenua* (country); *nui* (big). Plenty of land.

Whenuapai *whenua* (country); *pai* (good). Good land.

Whetūkura *whetū* (star); *kura* (red). Red star.

Whirinaki To lean, or the buttress of a house.

Whitianga The crossing, or the ford.

Appendix:
European place names

The following European names are mentioned in the text. The Māori names that follow may be the original names, or may contain a reference to the European place name in the text. Some suburbs that have Māori names are also listed under the cities.

Alum Creek
Waimangeo
Anderson's Bay
Puketai
Arrow River
Haehaenui
Kimiākau
Ashburton River
Hakatere
Aspiring, Mount
Tititea
Athens
Ātene
Auckland
Akarana
Kahu
Kohimārama
Kōhuaora
Māngere
Manukau
Manurewa
Maungakiekie
Mokoia
Ōnehunga
Ōtāhuhu
Ōwairaka

Papakura
Papatoetoe
Pupuke
Rangitoto
Remuera
Takapuna
Tāmaki
Tāmaki-makaurau
Taurangamangō
Taurarua
Te Kūrae-o-Tura
Te Pāpapa
Te Ranga-o-Taikehu
Te Tātua
Te Tō
Titirangi
Waiatarua
Waikomiti
Waitakere
Waitematā
Whau
Avon River
Ōrotore
Ōtākaro
Ōtautahi

Avondale
Whau
Balclutha
Iwikatea
Bay of Islands
Kahuwera
Kerikeri
Kororāreka
Motuarohia
Moturoa
Paihia
Pēowhairangi
Taiamai
Te Pēwhairangi
Tokerau
Bay View
Pētane
Ben Ohau
Aroaro-kaihe
Berea
Peria
Bethany
Pētane
Bethlehem
Peterehema

Bishop's Peninsula
  Huri-o-te-wai
Blenheim
  Waiharakeke
Bligh Sound
  Te Anahāwea
Blue Lake
  Tikitapu
Bluff
  Motupōhue
  Motupiu
Boulder Bank
  Te Pokohiwi
Bowen Falls
  Hine-te-awa
Breaksea Sound
  Huihui-kōura
Brewster, Mount
  Haumaitikitiki
Brothers, The
  Ngāwhatu
Brunner, Lake
  Kōtuku
  Moanakōtuku
Buller River
  Kawatiri
Burnett Range
  Kamautūrua
Cambridge
  Maungatautari
Camel, Mount
  Maungataniwha
Canaan
  Kenana
Canterbury Plains
  Ngā or Kā-pākihi-
  whakatekateka-a-
  Waitaha

Cargill, Mount
  Kapuka-tau-mohaka
Cass Bay
  Motukauatirahi
Cass River
  Horokōau
Castlecliff
  Kai-hau-o-Kupe
Castle Rock
  Motutere
Christchurch
  Aranui
  Kaiapoi
  Ōpawa
  Ōrotore
  Ōtākaro
  Ōtautahi
  Papanui
  Pūtaringamotu
Clarence River
  Waiautoa
Clutha River
  Kāhuika
  Matau
Colville, Cape
  Moehau
  Te Kupenga-a-
  Taramainuku
Cook, Mount
  Aoraki
  Aorangi
  Kirikiri-katata
Cook Strait
  Arahura
  Arapaoa
  Ngāwhatu
  Raukawa
  Te Tao-o-Kupe

Corinth
  Koriniti
Coromandel
  Motutere
  Tapu
  Whakatete
Corsair Bay
  Motukauatiiti
Croisilles Harbour
  Whangarae
Crown Range
  Haumaitikitiki
Curious Cove
  Kahikatea
Cyrene
  Hairini
Daggs Sound
  Te Rā
Damascus
  Ramaiku
Dannevirke
  Umutaoroa
D'Archiac, Mount
  Kāhuikaupeka
Devonport
  Te Kūrae-o-Tura
  Te Ranga-o-Taikehu
Dog Island
  Motupiu
Doubtful Sound
  Kāhuikākāpō
Dunedin
  Kaikōrai
  Ōpoho
  Ōtepoti
  Puketai
  Te Au
  Te Ika-a-Paraheke
  Wakāri

Dusky Sound	**Freeman's Bay**	**Hall's Arm**
Manutiti	Te Tō	Kāhuikākāpō
Motukiekie	**French Pass**	**Hamilton**
Tamatea	Te Aumiti	Kirikiriroa
East Cape	**Galatea**	**Hastings**
Tapuwaeroa	Karatia	Heretaunga
Edwardson Arm	**Galilee**	**Hawke Bay**
Moanawhenuapōuri	Kariri	Te Matau-a-Māui
Egmont, Mount	**Gisborne**	**Hen and Chicken**
Minarapa	Mangapapa	**Islands**
Tāhurangi	Tūranga	Te Kupenga-a-
Tamaahua	Tūranga-nui-a-Kiwa	Taramainuku
Taranaki	Waerenga-a-hika	**Holdsworth, Mount**
Ellesmere, Lake	**Glen Eden**	Taratahi
Kaikanohi	Waikomiti	**Howick**
Kaitorete	**Goat Island**	Ōwairoa
Ko-te-kete-ika-a-	Pūrakanui	**Hutt Valley**
Tutekawa	**Golgotha**	Epuni
Waihora	Korokata	Heretaunga
Eutychus	**Grassmere, Lake**	Moerā
Utiku	Kaparatehau	Naenae
Fairy Springs	**Great Barrier Island**	Petone
Te Puna-a-Tūhoe	Aotea	Pōmare
Farewell Spit	Aotearoa	Taitā
Onetahua	**Great Mercury Island**	Te Ahi-a-Manono
Featherston	Ahuahu	Waiwhetū
Kaiwaiwai	**Green Lake**	**Invercargill**
Feilding	Rotokākahi	Arowhenua
Aorangi	**Greymouth**	Waihopai
Five Rivers	Mawhera	Waikiwi
Aparima	**Grey River**	**Jackson's Head**
Flaxbourne	Mawhera	Kupenga-a-Kupe
Waiharakeke	Moutapu	Te Tao-o-Kupe
Forsyth, Lake	**Greytown**	**Jerusalem**
Ko-te-kete-ika-a-	Houhoupounamu	Hiruhārama
Tutekawa	**Grove Arm**	**Judea**
Wairewa	Iwirua	Te Hūria
Foveaux Strait	**Haast Pass**	**Judges Bay**
Ara-a-Kiwa	Tioripātea	Taurarua

Kidnappers, Cape
  Tapuwaeroa
King Country
  Rohepōtae
Laodicea
  Raorikia
Lawyers Head
  Te Ika-a-Parehika
Levin
  Horowhenua
Linton
  Te Kairanga
Little Barrier Island
  Hauturu
London
  Rānana
Lyall Bay
  Maranui
Lyttelton
  Ōketeupoko
  Te Whakaraupō
McKenzie Country
  Aorangi
McLaren's Peak
  Matapehi-o-te-rangi
Macedonia
  Makerōnia
Marton
  Tūtaenui
Mayor Island
  Tūhua
Mercury Harbour
  Whanganui-o-Hei
Milford Sound
  Piopiotahi
  Te Pari
Moonlight Gully
  Kā-kōhaka-ruru-whenua

Napier
  Ahuriri
  Hukarere
  Keteketerau
  Marewa
  Pānia
  Upokopōito
Nelson
  Horoirangi
  Koputīraha
  Maitai
  Tāhunanui
  Wakapuaka
  Wakatū
  Whakatū
New Plymouth
  Ngāmotu
  Paritutū
Nile River
  Waitakere
Normanby
  Ketemarae
North Cape
  Muriwhenua
North Island
  Eaheinomauwe
  He Ahi-nō-Māui
  Nukuroa
  Te Ika-a-Māui
One Tree Hill
  Maungakiekie
Pacific Ocean
  Te Moana-nui-a-Kiwa
Palliser, Cape
  Te Kawakawa
Palmerston North
  Awapuni
  Hokowhitu
  Papaioea

  Te Papaioea
Panmure
  Mokoia
Passage Island
  Motutawaki
Pelorus Sound
  Te Hoiere
Pepin Island
  Huri-o-te-wai
Philippi
  Piripai
Picton
  Waitohi
Port Chalmers
  Kopūtai
Port Levy
  Koukourarata
Port Nicholson
  Pōneke
  Te Whanganui-a-Tara
Prospect, Mount
  Haumaitikitiki
Providence, Cape
  Kōurariki
Pumpkin Flat
  Te Pāpapa
Quail Island
  Ōtamahua
Queen Charlotte Sound
  Arapaoa
  Motuora
Rainbow Mountain
  Maungakaramea
Riccarton
  Pūtaringamotu
Riverton
  Pūkorokio

Russell	Māhunui	**Weeks Island**
Kororāreka	Te Waipounamu	Puketutu
Maiki	Te Waka-a-Aoraki	**Wellington**
St John, Lake	Te Waka-a-Māui	Hātaitai
Waiatarua	**Spey River**	Karori
Samaria	Kāhuikākāpō	Makara, or Mākara
Hamaria	**Stevens Island**	Maranui
Scinde Island	Huihui-kōura	Mātairangi
Hukarere	**Stewart Island**	Muritai
Seatoun	Rakiura	Ngaio
Tūranga	Te Puka-a-Māui	Ngāuranga
Sefton, Mount	**Stop Island**	Ōhāriu
Aroaro-kaihe	Motukiekie	Ōhiro
Selwyn River	**Sumner, Lake**	Ōtari
Waikerikeri	Hakakura	Rongotai
Shag Point	**Tasman, Mount**	Te Aro
Ārai-te-uru	Horokōau	Te Kaminaru
Matakaea	**Tasman Sea**	Tinakori
Sheerdown, Mount	Moana-tāpokopoko-a-	Tūranga
Te Pari	Tāwhaki	**Wellington Harbour**
Shelly Beach	Tai-o-Rēhua	Hātaitai
Ōkā	**Teichelmann, Mount**	Matiu
Taurangamangō	Kirikiri-katata	Pōneke
Ship Cove	**Three Kings**	Te Whanganui-a-Tara
Meretoto	Te Tātua	**West Coast**
Silberhorn, Mount	**Three Kings Island**	Poutini
Kirikiri-katata	Manawatahi	Tai Poutini
Sinclair Head	**Tom Bowling Bay**	Te Ika-a-Māui
Rimurapa	Kapowairua	**Whale Island**
Smyrna	**Torlesse, Mount**	Moturātā
Hamurana	Whataarama	Moutohorā
Somes Island	**Victoria, Mount**	**White Island**
Matiu	Hātaitai	Whakaari
Southern Alps	**Warkworth**	**Wilton**
Kā-puke-māeroero	Mahurangi	Ōtari
South Island	Puhinui	**Young Nick's Head**
Arahura	**Watchman, The**	Te Kurī-a-Pawa
Arapaoa	Te Kupenga-	**Zion**
Kaikōura	a-Taramainuku	Hīona

Notes